Networking!

A STEP BY STEP GUIDE TO MASTERING NETWORKING
FOR BEGINNERS OR PROFESSIONALS, EVEN THE SHY & TIMID

KEN MARSH

Foreword by
Dr. Sandra Muse Kuhlmann

Inquiries should be sent to:
For Your Information Publications
11152 Westheimer #660
Houston, TX 77042, USA
www.FYIPress.com

E-mail: Kenpm50@aol.com
Website: www.fearlessnetworkers.com

Copy Editing and Final Proofing: Sandra Kuhlmann, Ph.D.:
www.fearlessnetworkers.com
Cover Design by: Kerry McFee: Minuteman Press Fort Bend:
www.fortbend.minutemanpress.com
Printing of paperback book by: Diginet Printing:
www.gperego@diginetprinting.com

First Printing 2004 (Awarded the 2004 Business Book of the Year by Houston Business Review)
Second Printing 2005

Library of Congress Catalog Card Number: 2004090668

Marsh, Kenneth P. Fearless Networking!: A Step-by-step Guide to Mastering Networking For Beginners and Professionals, Even the Shy & Timid
Includes Bibliography and Index

ISBN: 0-9749614-0-X
ISBN: 0-9749614-2-6 converted to 978-0-9749614-2-2

This book is available at a special discount when ordered in bulk quantities.

The author is available for seminars, interviews, consulting and speaking engagements.

Printed in the United States of America

To Sabrina, Je Taime, Roger and LaTonya
Thank you for surrounding me with love.

Praise for Fearless Networking!

I've known Ken Marsh for over 15 years, and he exemplifies what the philosophy of "Giver's Gain" is all about. The positive, uplifting impact he has had on my life because of his generosity of spirit is what he is writing about in Fearless Networking! Ken lives what he teaches and writes about. I strongly urge the reader to follow his sage advice!

> Marilyn Gardner, Vice President of Sales &
> Marketing Beazer Homes

What does this book offer for the seasoned networker? New ideas! A fresh approach! A clearer purpose in your work and in your networking! A willingness to take Ken's suggestion and test the law of reciprocity, give and you will receive. I have learned so much from working with this manuscript. It has become a part of who I am. I am a better person and professional through my exposure to Fearless Networking!

> Dr. Sandra M. Kuhlmann, Consultant, Training &
> Development Excerpt of Foreword to Fearless Networking

I've known Ken for over ten years. His is not a book about theories or abstract conceptualizations of interfacing successfully with fellow human beings. Ken's approach comes from experience as a master of networking successfully to achieve dreams by helping others achieve theirs. A timely work in this age of electronics, that ironically threatens to isolate us. Fearless Networking! is an antidote for the age we live.

> Richard Rosenthal, Director Bilingual
> Education Institute Houston

Networking is a subject given far too little attention and focus considering the impact it can have on your business's success (or failure). I feel that Ken's Fearless Networking book is long overdue! It is my hope that Ken's book will enjoy the same success as Donna Fisher's and Sandy Vilas' first book, "*Power Networking*."

John Younker, PhD
TEC (The Executive Committee) and
Associates In Continuous Improvement

The book in your hands is a gold mine for the business professional! Fearless Networking! so ably illustrates the joy of the Biblical principle: "Give and it shall be given to you." Ken Marsh is a man of integrity, grace and humility and has earned the right to talk about his subject like no one else can!

Jerry Twentier, Author
The Positive Power Of Praising People

FEARLESS NETWORKING! is a practical, easy-to-understand guide that will dramatically increase the number of referrals given and received by anyone who sincerely follows Ken's advice.

Dr. Ivan Misner, Founder & CEO
Business Network International (BNI)
co-author, best selling *Masters of Networking*

If you want to use networking as a way to grow your business, you need to know what Ken Marsh tells you in Fearless Networking!

Paul and Sarah Edwards, co-authors, best selling
Getting Business to Come to You

Fearless Networking!, emphasizes the importance of people in business. For business to succeed, the business owner must have the courage and know how to engage in vital networking activities. Fearless Networking! is a people book, a guide to building better and lasting relationships. Where there are people, there is business. Where there is business, there is promise! Where there is promise, there is prosperity! Fearless Networking! Is a must read for each business owner.

> Ola Joseph, Speaker & Consultant
> CEO of Riverbank & Associates
> Author of Soaring on the Wings of Courage, The
> Art of Self-Encouragement

FEARLESS NETWORKING! is a straight forward, how-to manual that provides exactly what you need to build a large network of people you can count on. While president of BNI-West University Chapter in Houston, Ken led by example and influenced hundreds of people with his consistently numerous referrals. His book, Fearless Networking!, expands this potential to positively impact networkers world-wide!

> Kathleen A. Mathy, CPA, Executive Director
> Business Network International (BNI)-Houston
> West Contributing Author, *Masters of Networking*

As a member of Ken's BNI West University chapter, I can attest to the fact that he has attained all that he says he has and more. More importantly, however, is the inspiration he has provided our chapter. Many authors talk the talk but few walk the talk as Ken has. His book Fearless Networking! is indeed a special legacy to us all!

> Bill Pellerin, President, Texas Investigative Services
> Licensed Private Investigator

Fearless Networking!

Table of Contents

ix

Disclaimer Notice

This e-book publication is being distributed with the expressed and implied understanding that the author and publisher are not engaged in rendering legal, accounting or other professional advice.
If legal advice or other expert assistance is required, the services of a competent professional should be sought. While the author has made every effort to be factual, your results may vary.

FOREWORD
by
Sandra Kuhlmann, Ph.D.

I am a timid networker, one that comes up with excuses to stay away from those networking events. So when I read Ken's title, I was hooked. The introduction gave me encouragement. There is hope out there for those of us who lack confidence to network! Next, I scanned the 24 topics that cover the key issues of successful networking. I was motivated and could feel my comfort zone loosing its tight grasp. I was more hopeful. The book looked simple enough that I was compelled to read on. I trust that this will be the same for you, the reader!

What does this book offer that other books on networking don't? Fearless Networking is a more concise description and plan for networking. The book has a simple system, that even the fearful, can embrace. The Ken Marshisms make the book unique and powerful. Part of the uniqueness of the work is the focus on Fearless Networking. This is a strength of the book and sets it apart from others.

This book has lots of possibilities and a wide audience. The book reveals a complex process in simple steps. The process is totally directed at circumventing the fear and insecurity barriers of networking. It is a valuable book for organizations that have sales representatives. It is perfect for the small business owner. It is a wonderful text for teaching and training. It is a must read for people in today's uncertain business market.

What does this offer for the seasoned networker? New ideas! A fresh approach! A clearer purpose in your work and in your networking. A willingness to take Ken's suggestion and test the law of reciprocity. Give and you will receive. I have learned so much from working with this manuscript. It has become a part of who I am. I am a better person and professional through my exposure to Fearless Networking!

Ken is a stellar example of this program. He has earned the right to write this book.

The book is filled with creative ideas and tips. Ken has a positive way of expressing himself that gives networkers and non-networkers the motivation to get going. This book also delivers what it promises. The book is already a success. Ken has given so much of himself and his organization over the years. I hope this book will give back to Ken Marsh some shred of what he has given to others.

Introduction

Fearless Networking! A priceless guide designed to boost your confidence when business networking and developing mutual win-win relationships. Also, it is a way to increase market penetration for your product or service. Whether you are a shy and timid networker or a seasoned master networker, this book provides you with the "how to" tools and techniques to self-direct your way to greater success and fortune. Besides helping you increase market penetration and earn more money, you will most certainly receive the inner joy and satisfaction that comes from *unselfish* service to others. Never again will you be deterred by a lack of assertion and confidence when offering your network's service or product to a prospect or client. At your fingertips and at the tip of your tongue, you will have practical tips that will dramatically increase the number of referrals you give and receive. You will develop mutually beneficial relationships with an ever-increasing number of people in your network!

Fearless Networking! Ensures that the dialogue you use with prospects and clients is on target, positive and results-oriented. This manual provides over two hundred solutions to problems networkers face on a daily basis. Especially those of you, who are held back from networking by fear, will benefit!

Fearless Networking! Is the most inspiring, practical and professional resource available to all who desire to grow their business primarily by networking. Those business people who practice the ideas in this book will expand their network of influence. In addition they will experience the personal satisfaction that comes from being a "go-giver"!

Fearless Networking! Provides results-oriented networking tracts that elicit new business for you and your network. The process identifies prospect/client concerns and challenges. Then provides a roadmap to successfully grow the business. The manual is easy to use and recall; i.e., incorporates acronyms, quick summaries, repetition of key words/phrases, and mind-pictures.

Fearless Networking! Is for business owners, executives or sales professionals who do not have the time for research and study to increase their market share. The book provides solutions for you and your network today! Are the answers buried in a CD or audiotape? Lost in the pages of a motivational book, buried deep in your files, or gathering dust on some shelf reserved for seminar notes? The best place for these seminal ideas is where you can quickly find them – in your memory, on the tip of your tongue. For those who believe they have a poor memory, I allow no such excuse. The material is designed to aid recall and retention. Several checklists are available to use for self-improvement and self-motivation. Finally, an index of tracts and tips is conveniently organized, for quick access, by categories for use when under stress, prior to, during, and after networking events.

Here's to happy and fearless networking!

Special Bonus Section

Four Attitudes

Before I give you a few tips on how to use this manual for optimum benefit, I must first talk about four attitudes related to networking. Three of these attitudes create obstacles on the road to fearless networking. One of these attitudes will overcome the obstacles and open new doors for you and your business.

Attitude #1: Close-minded

Some people are close-minded to new ways of doing business. They believe that their way is best. Others are reluctant to try something different. They are comfortable with their way, even if they are not getting the results they want. Others will half-heartedly try new ways to prove that the different way won't work. They are their own worst enemy. They are not willing to let go of the old to grasp the new or different.

What to do if you are close-minded:

Make a decision to utilize the new or different way as recommended for 30 days. Then compare results of the new ideas to the results of the old ideas.

Attitude #2: Compliance

Some people are open to new ideas and are inspired by what they have read. They are not, however, committed to use the suggestions presented for the long-term. Some fail because of laziness, others because they are afraid of success or failure. Still others blame a poor memory, a busy schedule or finances. Also there may be those who are overwhelmed by so many tools they don't know where to begin.

What to do if you have an attitude of compliance:

Identify your priorities. Then make time to read the suggestions of your favorite chapter. Utilize the quick summary, the objectives and action plan. Reflect how the chapter you chose can help you get on the right road to fearless networking. Once you have done this, follow the action plans. Enjoy the results of giving and serving others. Motivation follows action! Not the other way around!

Attitude #3: Driven by Worry or Fear

Worry is a habit for some people. They may be driven by fear. People with the fear and worry attitude *need* to achieve their monthly sales quota or business volume. They view the fearless networking concept, building relationships and helping others, too slow a process. They will wait to try these concepts when sales or business improves. In other words, never!

What to do when you are driven by worry or fear:

First, deal with your worry or fear by reading the Dale Carnegie book, *How to Stop Worrying and Start Living.* Find a worry principle that will help with your worry or fears. Second, discover that your worry or fear is drastically reduced when you focus on helping others and not on your problems. Finally, realize that worry or fear is the enemy. Fearless networking is your friend. Worry or fear can sap your energy, rob you of your creative abilities and sabotage your commitment to succeed.

More importantly, worry or fear can cause you to appear needy or desperate. Both are counterproductive to new business development. Join a BNI networking group in your area or start one. Soon you will have 20, 30 or 40 people network marketing your products or services for you. What you have to do is develop a winning 60 seconds product/service presentation and give the presentation, once a week, to your marketing team. This is a way to take the pressure off!

4

Attitude #4: Commitment

The great description of commitment is the story of the chicken and the pig. You may have heard the story. Please indulge me anyway. One day the chicken and pig were walking down the street. The chicken noticed a billboard advertisement for breakfast. The display included a picture of a plate with 2 eggs and 3 strips of bacon. The hen began bragging about the labor she had to put forth to furnish eggs for breakfast. The pig said, I appreciate your contribution to this fine meal. Take a look at the bacon. For you it's all in a day's work. For me it is total commitment! Some will read this "how to," become committed and take action on the practical tools and tips.

What to do when you have an attitude of commitment:

Maintain that attitude by keeping company with others of a similar attitude! Realize that negatives are ten times more powerful than positives. When you happen to be in the company of negative people, answer the bad with good and the negative with positive. Stay away from negative pity parties. Smile and keep on giving and serving.

Why use this manual

This manual provides you with powerful referral tracts, tools and tips. The proposals drastically reduce shyness, timidity, nervousness and fear prior to, during and after a business-networking event. Boost your confidence. Increase your effectiveness in building win-win relationships. Practice what Dr. Ivan Misner, founder and CEO, Business Network International, calls "givers gain." Givers gain means that the good you do comes back to help you in ways you cannot foresee. For the master or professional networker, this "how to" manual will assist you in enhancing your already sound abilities.

The manual provides you the proper tools, to overcome challenges, maintain relationships and hold you accountable to do what you must to continue building wealth and success. This manual encourages you to give and serve without expecting something in return. When you serve your network by providing referrals to help grow their business, you establish lasting relationships. Trust this way of doing business! Have a positive expectancy that the universe will reciprocate in kind!

How to use this manual:

This collection of powerful networking techniques is organized by chapters. You must read the first three chapters first so you will understand the philosophy. You can read the other chapters in what order is most important to you and your work. They can be studied alone or in combination with other chapters. The chapters are designed for easy reading and recall of the practical tools and tips. The materials include a motivational saying, short introduction, and a quick summary. The information has memory aids, such as acronyms, stacking techniques and quick summaries. The other chapters can be selectively read based on areas of interest or need.

Also, remember that these powerful networking tools will work in other networking areas such as networking for a job, for finding a significant other, for Kingdom building/evangelizing, and for identifying a mentor. Your "Ideal Customer" (See 60 seconds presentation in Chapter 10) will become your "Ideal Prospect" relative to the networking areas mentioned above.

At the end of each chapter are learning objectives for knowledge, skill, attitude and behavior changes. Each chapter has an action plan that allows for immediate use of the tools and techniques, in the real world. Finally, a plus delta analysis tool is included. This tool comes from Dr. John Younker, TEC Chair. The plus delta (+□) analysis helps you ascertain (+) what went well and (□) what could be improved and how.

A Word about Using Memory Techniques:

This manual contains several memory boosters to help the recall and retention of the networking tips and tracts. Each memory booster will be denoted by a 💡 symbol.

Stacking Technique:

This memory technique requires several run-through practices to recall the key words and phrases of the mind-picture. Be sure to use the specific objects described for each memory stack with all the recommended color, action and exaggeration. This aids retention and recall. Once you have committed the mind-picture (objects) to memory, review the meaning of the referral tract provided. Challenge yourself to recall the meaning as you go through the mind-picture (objects) at least five times or until you can repeat the stack, from memory, from top to bottom and vice versus.

Acronyms:

The great thing about acronyms is the ease of recall of the meanings because the acronym usually has only 4 to 7 letters. Practice recalling the meanings associated with the acronym letters at least five times for quick recall and retention.

Making a New Start as a Fearless Networker!

Even if you're a shy and timid networker with a fear or dread concerning approaching a prospect or a seasoned networker, these four steps to making a new start will be of real benefit to your success as a business networker.

Step #1: Assume responsibility for where you are as a networker.

> You can choose how you deal with the stress, anxiety and fear about networking. Choose to follow the tracts, tips and philosophy of networking provided in this "how to" manual.

Step #2: Believe you can change and don't give up.

> No matter how reluctant you are to network if you believe in your heart you can change, you can. Take small steps initially and reward yourself even when you feel you've only made a small contribution at a networking event like being friendly and giving sincere praise to people you meet. Be persistent in attending

networking functions and using the tracts and tips provided to make connections with other attendees.

Step #3: Clarify your goal for the number of contacts you will make.

Make sure your goal is clear, specific, measurable, realistic (attainable) and time-bound.
For example: I will make a connection with one person tonight by following the first ten steps of the fifteen-step tract "A Proven Networking Tract For Beginners and Professionals, Even the Shy and Timid."

Step #4: Don't wait to begin.

Trust the tools provided they have worked for thousands of others in our seminars. Use the easy to follow techniques of the first three chapters, especially having a mind-set of "What can I give or contribute to this networking event?" and the "Self-Affirmation Talk."

Having information on how to excel at business networking at the forefront of your mind and at the tip of your tongue will help you to become a fearless networker in a very short time!

Fearless networkers confidently reach out to make connections with others.

Ten Traits of Fearless Networkers

"You will never leave where you are until you decide where you want to be."

--Lewis Dunnington

Fearless Networkers:

1. Desire to give to others.
2. Actively listen for needs, issues and concerns.
3. Are centered on others, rather than centered on themselves.
4. Value being held accountable by others.
5. Listen 80%; talk 20% when communicating with referrals. If you talk for more than 60 seconds after being asked a question, you're probably talking too much.
6. Understand the Universal Law of Reciprocity; give and you will receive. Recognize this as a Biblical or Spiritual principle.
7. Think about what they can give rather than what they can get.
8. Practice patience with prospects.
9. Reach out to others to make a connection.
10. Network fearlessly!

Before going further, let's evaluate ourselves as networkers. Let's assess how we rate as fearless networkers. For example, **how consistent is our behavior?**

Be honest now. No one will see this but you. No one is grading this. A promotion is not riding on your score. There are no right and wrong answers. This manual is a great mirror to view our networking behavior. So let's get an honest appraisal of where you are right now. We will repeat this exercise after you have finished working through this manual.

On a scale of 1 to 10 (10 is excellent and 1 is awful), circle a number that best describes you as a networker. Tell your spouse, boss, teacher, mom or dad that it is highly suggested that you write in this book! Unless you may have borrowed it or plan to give it to someone in your network!

Pre Self-Evaluation

I desire to give to others much more than finding business for myself:
1   2   3   4   5   6   7   8   9   10

I actively listen for needs, issues and concerns when face-to-face with a prospect:
1   2   3   4   5   6   7   8   9   10

I reach out to others and am not a wallflower I do not loiter around the bar or food table:
1   2   3   4   5   6   7   8   9   10

I seek to build a relationship before delving into my product/opportunity spiel (I spend 90% of my time in rapport building, identifying common interests, needs identification and 5% on my own presentation):
1   2   3   4   5   6   7   8   9   10

I listen 80% and talk 20% when communicating with a prospective referral:
1   2   3   4   5   6   7   8   9   10

I think of my network when face-to-face with a prospective referral:
1   2   3   4   5   6   7   8   9   10

I work a room with poise and confidence:
1   2   3   4   5   6   7   8   9   10

I reach out to others to make a connection and am not just a card-dropper:
1   2   3   4   5   6   7   8   9   10

I am a **Fearless Networker!**
1   2   3   4   5   6   7   8   9   10

That wasn't so bad, was it? At the end of this manual you will rate yourself again so you can record your progress toward becoming a **Fearless Networker!**

About the Author

"People don't care how much you know until they know how much you care."
-Zig Ziglar

Kenneth P. Marsh is CEO of Fearless Networking, Inc. He has been a business owner specializing in the relationship-building arena since 1993. He was formerly Director of Training for one of the world's largest for-profit training organizations. Ken has authored more than 70 titles including over 40 titles on business networking alone. He is also, a contract instructor for Tomball College. Ken has also developed curriculum for Rice University School of Business. He has given many motivational presentations as keynote speaker and guest speaker, and has been the recipient of numerous speaking awards.

Ken is the Past President of the American Society for Training and Development-Houston Chapter. He is a business show advisor for CNN AM650. Ken writes a weekly article titled "Marsh's Mantras: Words to Build a Network and Life" for HoustonBusiness.Com.

The first printing of this book, "Fearless Networking!" received a "Business Book of the Year" for 2004 from Houston Business Review.

Ken is a graduate of Lamar University. He spent 15 years of his early career utilizing his educational background as a computer programmer, systems analyst, project supervisor, general accounting supervisor, and information systems manager before becoming a trainer, training director, executive coach, job-fit consultant, business owner and author.

Chapter 1

My Philosophy of Networking

"Live according to your highest light and more light will be given you."

-Peace Pilgrim

"Although we often give goods, favors and appreciation or attention in order to receive something in return, the universe reminds us that whatever we most need is what we most need to give."

-Anonymous

The journey on the road to becoming fearless networkers, even for the shy and timid, begins by defining business networking. First, let's define what business networking isn't.

Business networking isn't:
- Dropping your card in a prize bowl at your favorite restaurant hoping to win a free meal
- Handing out your business card to anyone who will accept it
- Creating a list of people to call in hopes of selling to them
- Putting everyone who has given you a card on your electronic newsletter e-mail distribution list without a follow up program
- Tacking your card on the bulletin board at your local retailer
- Introducing yourself or being introduced to another person and not exploring a business relationship
- Prospecting to get personal leads

Now, let's look at what business networking is.

Business networking is:
- Acquiring a database of diverse people, with diverse products and services, who understand and practice "give and take"
- Developing mutually beneficial win-win relationship with others
- Giving, pure and simple!
- Relationship building with the intent to eventually share referrals
- Promoting you and your good reputation
- Building quality business relationships where there is ease, comfort, reliability and respect
- Serving others without expecting anything in return
- Being confident that the same people you are serving, in time, will serve you in return

What is serving or giving?

Giving, serving and service are the foundation of true business networking. An excellent explanation of service or serve comes from the book by Ron McCann, *"The Joy of Service."* "If you don't like the word service or serve, it's probably because the words have assumed a very negative connotation. Both come from the Latin word *servus,* which means, "slave." You can let go of that thought right now. People who serve are not slaves. Slaves are forced to do what people tell them.

People who serve choose to serve. When you begin to provide service because you choose to, out of joy, everything transforms. You no longer look at customers as people with money…. suddenly they are people who need something…suddenly you are a friend who can help them. You create a relationship when you serve them, and through that service experience, they serve you. A lot of creativity is required to begin, establish and maintain that type of relationship. That is where the joy of serving comes into play. Here's a thought for you to consider--maybe relationships are active only *while* we are serving one another."

The willingness to serve

I once was shy and timid as a networker. The major contributing factor to my success, as a fearless business networker is my willingness to serve. I want to help members of my network grow their businesses. This sincere desire to serve is how I personally have built long-term relationships with 80% of my business client base.

For example, I am more than a very effective trainer for my clients. I am the number one problem solver on their team! Several years ago, one of my clients, an owner of a 57 year old manufacturing company in Houston, was hours away from purchasing a $120,000 CNC Lathe. When informed of the purchase, I called members in my network in manufacturing. I inquired as to whether this was a good deal for him. After I received information about a better plan, I phoned and told him that there was a way to save him money on the same type of equipment, a different name brand yet one of equal or better quality with refurbished special add-on equipment and with the same warranty. He was interested. He cleared some time on his calendar that day. I picked him up in my Jeep and drove him to the two companies I mentioned in my call. The happy ending was that my client saved $60,000. He got the machine he wanted, with all the special add-on equipment of the new one he was about to purchase. This client has been happy with the performance of his purchase for almost three years.

My client was extremely pleased with the sales and customer service training my company has provided his company for more than eight years. I did not see our relationship as being only a provider of quality training. I was also his number one problem solver. During my long tenure with this same client, I helped him acquire a business loan. I assisted him in writing a business plan, completing his financial documents and working with his CPA. I helped him hire a General Manager and develop a compensation plan for his sales team and a gain sharing plan for his plant staff. Recently, I have been assisting him, through my extensive network database, in relocating his company.

Here is another example of bringing value-added service to my clients through my network. One of my long-term clients of nine years, owner of a profitable rubber hose distribution company, was in search of a new president for his company. He asked for my support during the decision making process. Once the decision was made, the owner announced to his fellow TEC members that he was very appreciative of the advice I provided. He said that I was one of two people he respected enough to seek advice on this critical matter. The outcome was that he selected the person I supported. He eventually sold the company to this person.

A Life of Giving Back

Writing *Fearless Networking!* has allowed me to take inventory of what I give to the community. I believe those in leadership positions should give back to the community. Here are some ways that I have done that.

I am the immediate past president of the Rotary Club of Sharpstown (Houston). Our club is part of the largest service organization in the world, 1.2 million Rotarians, Rotary International (RI). RI provides programs on literacy and education, health prevention, polio eradication in third world countries, immunization of children locally, nationally and international, and poverty alleviation on a local, national and international basis.

I am chair of District 5890 (56 clubs) Rotary Youth Leadership Awards program where upwards of 100 youth are given scholarships to attend a 3-day leadership training camp each year. I provide leadership training to the District 5890 Rotary Interact youth leaders. I am a member of the Rotary District 5890 Interact committee.

I am also a mentor for Project Hope, a mentoring program for "at-risk" youth at Lee High School which is a highly, ethnically diverse magnet school in the Houston Independent School District (HISD). I have adopted Homeroom 7C at YES College Preparatory School, a nationally acclaimed private school whose mission is to prepare "at-risk" students for a four-year college education. Finally, I am a volunteer facilitator for the Success At Work (SAW) program. SAW is a program for middle school students to learn about the job market, interview skills, teamwork, credit, and the entrepreneurial process.

16

Never Serve Alone

To become a fearless business networker, select the organizations that will provide the best core of networkers who value giving! I selected BNI, the world's largest networking organization (55,000 members in the U.S. and 16 countries). Belonging to BNI is like having dozens of sales people working for me. Members carry your business cards with them. When they meet a prospect, they hand out your card and recommend you.

It's as simple as that! It's based on the proven concept of BNI founder and CEO, Dr. Ivan Misner, called "givers gain." If I give you business, you'll give me business. We'll both benefit as a result. Last year (2003), members of BNI passed over two million referrals. This generated hundreds of millions of dollars (U.S.) worth of business. BNI is a business and professional networking organization that allows only one person per professional classification or specialty to join a chapter. I am a past president of the BNI West University Chapter, one of 25 such chapters in the greater Houston area. Since becoming a member more than two years ago, I have received the "Most Notable Networker" award for 33 consecutive months for the "Most Referrals"! I'm proud to say that I give an average of 22 referrals a month, one every business day, to my BNI chapter members. (See www.bni.com)

Another organization that is a key to my success is The Executive Committee (TEC) Associate's Round Table (T.A.R.T.). Before I explain what T.A.R.T. is and my role in this organization, I must familiarize you with the TEC organization. TEC's mission is "increasing the effectiveness and enhancing the lives of chief executives." TEC members meet once a month to work *on* their business, not *in* their business. They find solutions using the collective experience of 15 peer chief executives and business owners, all on the firing line every day. TEC has 8,624 members in 12 countries and 86 cities across the U.S. Each TEC group is led by a TEC Chair, an experienced businessperson who runs or has run a successful business.

The T.A.R.T. members are providers of services to the chief executives of TEC. The T.A.R.T. members often recommend members of their network to TEC members. My T.A.R.T. Chair, Dr. John Younker, is one of the founding TEC Chairs in the Houston area. Dr. Younker has a deep abiding respect for each member's personal and business life. He holds us accountable for results. It is comforting to have someone with the experience and qualifications of Dr. Younker in your corner, especially for those tough times, both business and personal. Dr. Younker has a wealth of knowledge and experience. He helps chief executives and business owners and professionals live successful lives. My T.A.R.T. group is more than a networking group. They are a group of top-notch professionals and business people who freely give from their experiences. I have included associates in TEC and T.A.R.T. in my database of trusted, respected and reliable business networkers. (See TEC at www.teconline.org)

Another world-class organization that has influenced my philosophy about service is Dale Carnegie & Associates, Inc. Dale Carnegie & Associates, Inc., is one of the largest for-profit training organizations in the world. Dale Carnegie Training® has created generations of successful business people. They believe that the success of organizations depends on the success of individuals.

I was an Instructor of seven Dale Carnegie® courses, instructor trainer and Director of Training in Houston, TX, and Washington D.C. I lived the philosophy Mr. Carnegie embodied in the 30 human relations principles found in the timeless masterpiece of *How to Win Friends and Influence People*. Mr. Rick Jones, President of Leadership Excellence, Inc., and Dale Carnegie Sponsor in Houston, provided me a life changing experience. From this opportunity I was able to springboard into a life of service. Mr. Jones is a superb salesperson, motivator. He believes in excellence in training materials and delivery. He develops strong sales teams. Leadership Excellence, Inc., is dedicated to tailoring programs to meet the needs of the client and building long-term relationships. I recommend people in my network take a Dale Carnegie Course® to help lead more prosperous and successful lives.

My mentor at Dale Carnegie & Associates, Inc., in Houston, TX was Sandra Muse Kuhlmann, Ph.D. She has been with this organization for over twenty years. Dr. Kuhlmann, a consultant in training and development, is the epitome of class, humility in service and leadership. She believed in me and gave me a clearer vision of servicing others and making a difference. To understand how to serve with humility and dignity, take the Dale Carnegie Course®. The return on investment exceeds the initial investment! (Visit www.dale-carnegie.com)

Oprah's Secret of Success

Oprah Winfrey credits her wealth to her spirit of giving. She believes in the Universal Law of Reciprocity, give and you will receive. Aside from surprising her studio audience several times a year with a million dollars in gifts, Oprah has an Angel Network that allows her worldwide audience to be "Angel Investors." They invest money, books, food, clothing, and sweat equity in helping the needy at home and abroad! What's the return on investment? According to Oprah, she is blessed with more money than she could ever spend! She demonstrates heartfelt enthusiasm when she gives to others, like a kid opening presents at holiday time. You, too, can be an "Angel Investor." Help members of your network grow their businesses. You will reap the rewards of *unselfish* giving. You will be blessed with more business. You will experience joy and genuine enthusiasm.

I am an "Angel Investor!" Ten percent of the royalties from my book *Fearless Networking!* will go to the Spirit of Life Community Church for the "Angel Mission for At-Risk Youth." A local community program designed as a destructive behavior intervention for youth at-risk of completing their education, falling prey to abuse, drug or alcohol addiction or other moral compromises including teen pregnancy, gang activity and crime.

Quick Summary:

Networking is relationship building with the intent of sharing referrals.

Objectives:

1. To get to know people by becoming genuinely interested in them
2. To recognize their need for help
3. To show them how you and/or your network can help fill the need
4. To remember that people refer people to people they know, like, trust and respect

Action Plan: 💡

1. Develop an attitude of service.
2. Be willing to serve *unselfishly*.
3. Join a quality referral-sharing, business networking group.
4. Look for ways to make a connection with others and develop a business relationship.
5. Find an inspiring mentor.
6. Join a peer business advisory group dedicated to enhancing the lives and increasing the effectiveness of chief executives and professionals (e.g., TEC or T.A.R.T.).
7. Take a Dale Carnegie Course® and learn skills to become a more effective, success-driven leader in your business/professional and personal life.

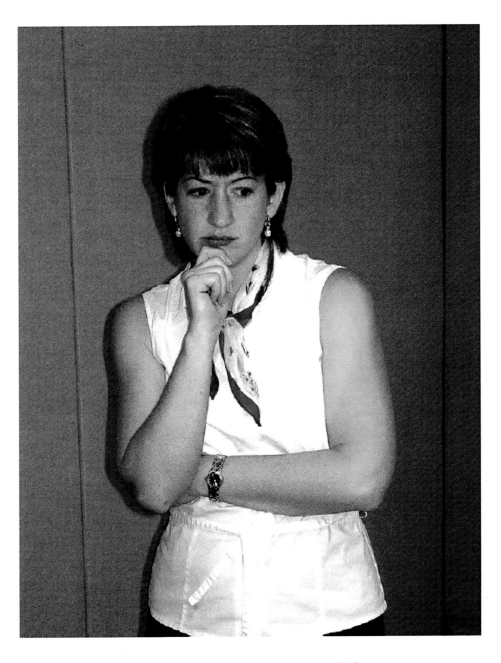

Is stress, anxiety or fear holding you back?

Chapter 2

Taking the Stress, Anxiety and Fear Out Of Attending Networking Events

"The best way of overcoming fear is taking action and doing what you fear most."

-Dale Carnegie

Has this ever happened to you? You find yourself dreading a networking event. As the day of the event draws near, you come up with several valid reasons not to attend. You remember your commitment to spend more time with your kids. You might go for a little while. Your head aches. You're feeling uncomfortable. Your mouth feels dry.

You don't like to talk about yourself. You have to talk about your product and services. You have to get someone to meet you after the event. So you can sell them! This is not worth it! Too much trouble! Too much stress! Better not go this time, after all.

The real reason for staying away from the networking event is unexplained anxiety and debilitating fear.

A Sure-Fire Way to Fearless Networking

A sure-fire way of taking the stress, anxiety and fear out of attending networking events is to change your objective for attending. If your objective for attending is based on, "What's in it for me?" you will be stressed. This is due to the pressure to perform or sell. We will explore this idea more and its impact on creating a negative experience.

If your objective is, "What can I give?" you will be more relaxed and confident. You can have more fun. You will leave with a pleasant reflection about the networking event. Possibly even looking forward to the next event! We will explore this idea also and its impact on creating a positive experience.

Let's explore more about having an attitude and behavior of "What's In It for Me?" or "What Can I Give?" What is its impact on your success or lack of success when attending a networking function?

"What Is in It for Me?" Attitude

When attending a networking function with this self-centered attitude, often you send a defeatist message. You need to meet your sales quota, make your bonus, keep your job, or get your business out of the red. You are sending the message that you need rescuing. This neediness and dependency, even unspoken, tends to repel, not attract!

Your behavior is focused on what the other people attending this event can do for you. Be aware of the negative impact:

"What Is in It for Me?" Behavior

- Talking more about your product and services while doing very little listening
- Making sure that everyone receives your business card
- Spending an inordinate amount of time with the people you came with or already know
- Hoping they will introduce you to a great prospect
- Standing near the refreshments waiting for someone to approach you
- Trying to impress and persuade others
- Criticizing yourself and others silently
- Telling yourself and others this is a waste of time

"What Can I Give?" Behavior

When attending a networking function and focusing on others, you are sending the message that you care. You want to contribute to the event. One of my favorite sayings is, "People don't care how much you know until they know how much you care." Caring tends to attract, not repel. When your objective is sincerely based on how you can contribute at this networking function, your behavior shows that you genuinely care. Another favorite saying is by Mary Kay Ash of Mary Kay Cosmetics "Fear can only settle in when our focus is inward. Take your mind off of

23

yourself and strive to help others and when you've helped enough other people reach their goals, you'll find that you have reached your own."
Positive behaviors are:

- Asking penetrating questions and actively listening for the needs/challenges of those you come in contact with
- Displaying a genuine interest and respect for the people you meet
- Referring someone in your network with care and delight
- Handing out your business card only when you have made a genuine connection
- Appearing relaxed, friendly and confident
- Having people come to you because they sense you care
- Contributing an uplifting comment, smile and attitude even when you have not made a referral
- Reflecting on contributing in some small way to the success of the event
- Looking forward to the next event and inquiring about the date and time of the next one

Quick Summary: 💡

A way of taking the stress, anxiety and fear out of networking functions is to change your reason for attending. Change from an attitude and behavior of "What's in for me?" to "What can I give or contribute?"

Objectives: 💡
1. To have an attitude of giving or serving others at all networking events you attend
2. To keep your network at the forefront of your mind
3. To recommend a member to help fill a need

Action Plan: 💡

1. Before a networking event or meeting, focus on how you can contribute and not on what you can receive.

2. Remember Zig Ziglar's saying, "You can get everything you want out of life by helping enough other people get what they want."
3. Refrain from talking too much about your business. A rule of thumb is 80% listening and 20% talking.
4. Find out about the other person's business issues, needs or challenges.
5. In a networking situation begin with your 60 seconds product/service presentation.
6. Conduct your fact-finding of the other person's product/service, company/industry information.
7. To discern wants from needs, actively listen for supporting evidence for each issue, need or challenge mentioned. Not getting evidence? Ask, "Why would you say that?"
8. Think of, who in your network can help overcome the issues, needs or challenges.
9. Give yourself a self-affirmation talk, visualizing taking action to serve others.
10. Conduct a $+\triangle$ analysis after the event or meeting to ascertain what went well and what you could have changed to be less stressful and anxious at the networking event.

Chapter 3

The Power of Self-Affirmations

"As far goes your self-direction, as far goes your freedom."

-Maria Ebner Von Eschenbach

My favorite way to increase my confidence before, during and after a networking event is to give myself a self-affirmation talk. I build my assertiveness by tailoring my talks for the event. Early in my career, I learned that using someone else's affirmation had little impact. The popular, "Day by day in every way, I'm getting better and better!" did not overcome my timidity. I was still nervous when I approached people at networking events. The reason for this is simple. Those words were not my own words. They grew out of someone else's goals and needs. Therefore, I doubted them!

One way I learned, how to overcome my reluctance came from my Dale Carnegie® experience. We learned how to build and deliver a self-direction talk to achieve our goals. The power of the self-talk was the positive, enthusiastic words and visualizations. Today, when I'm about to conduct a needs discovery with a prospective referral, I give myself a tailored self-affirmation talk. I emphasize two points: (1) This technique always boosts my confidence and courage. (2) I use this technique, when I'm not nervous or fearful. It gives me that edge to do my best job!

When I conduct workshops in anger management, handling angry or irate people, handling sales objections, and dealing with difficult people, I teach the participants to develop a self-affirmation talk. This technique helps maintain emotional control in contentious situations. In 6-months post workshop evaluations, the chief benefit of the training is the self-affirmation talk. So take this idea! Apply it! Enjoy the rewards!

The Elements of a Self-Affirmation Talk:

A = Attitude

B = Behavior

S = Situation

O = Objective

R = Recent Similar Situations

B = Bottom-line Results

How to Deliver a Self-Affirmation Talk

Ask yourself:
A = Attitude = What attitude do I want to have in this situation? Is it confidence? Poise? Enthusiasm? Self-direction?

B = Behavior = What behavior do I want to exhibit during this situation? Is it assertiveness? Confronting with care? Being outgoing?

S = Situation = What is the situation? Is it a business-networking event? Initial meeting with referral? Proposal/Action plan meeting?

State in a positive, enthusiastic manner:
O = Objective = I am maintaining an attitude of confidence and self-direction. My behavior says I am confronting with care, being assertive and displaying a genuine interest. Note: The A.B.S. (Attitude, Behavior, Situation) of the acronym A.B.S.O.R.B. is in the O. (Objective). The Self-affirmation talk begins by stating the O. (Objective); and continues with R. (Recent similar situations); ends with the B. (Bottom-line results)

R = Recent Similar Situations = I know I can do this! I did it before in the following similar situations: Note: Situations must be real-life situations that happened to you. For example:

1. I confronted the principal at Lee High School with care about starting an Interact club.
2. I was assertive in my business class when I role-played a problem solving session.
3. I showed a genuine interest when I mentored a new Rotarian about our community service projects.

B = Bottom-line Results: I have reached my goal of connecting with three people. I used the five-key steps toward becoming a fearless networker. I feel terrific!

Remember! Use the power of visualization while you give your self-affirmation talk:
Start visualizing while positively and enthusiastically saying the words in the O.R.B. portion of A.B.S.O.R.B. silently to yourself. See yourself maintaining an attitude of confidence and self-direction. Be sure your behavior confronts with care and shows genuine interest connecting with people. Visualize yourself in recent similar situations where you had a similar attitude and demeanor. Finally, in reference to the bottom-line results, see yourself connecting with others by using the five-key steps toward becoming a fearless networker. At the same time, see yourself feeling terrific. Putting feeling into your visualization along with positive attitude and behavior ensures a repeat of a successful performance!

Example self-affirmation talk for those who experience anxiety prior to networking:
The actual self-affirmation talk is the O.R.B. Visualize yourself behaving exactly like your words say. Walk the talk!
O. I am maintaining an attitude of self-confidence. My behavior demonstrates calmness, caring and listening with genuine interest. I concentrate on attendees at this Chamber of Commerce business after-hours event.

R. I know I can do this because I was:
1. Confident, calm and genuinely interested at a baby shower of a co-worker
2. Confident, caring and listening with genuine interest during a sales presentation at ABC Polymer Company
3. Genuinely interested in approaching and talking with visitors after church this past Sunday.

B. In return, I am receiving genuine interest from people at the event. I'm connecting with those at this Chamber of Commerce business after-hours event. I see myself, afterward jotting information on the reverse side of the business card I received from a prospective referral!

Quick Summary:

A personalized self-affirmation talk is a great way to ease nervousness and increase assertiveness in a business-networking event.

Objectives:

1. To prepare a self-affirmation talk following the format provided for each networking event or meeting for the next 90 days
2. To use the power of visualization while delivering your personalized self-affirmation talk
3. To use the O.R.B. and including the A.B.S. in your O.R.B.

Action Plan:

1. Prepare a practice self-affirmation talk.
2. Use a tape player or camcorder as you practice delivering your talk out loud.
3. Plan to attend several networking events during the month. Note: Check with your local Chamber for networking events and new member ribbon cutting events.
4. Conduct several $+\triangle$ analyses to ascertain what went well in your practice sessions and what went well at the networking event. Also, in all sessions ascertain what you could have improved or changed for a

better result.

MEMORY BOOSTER 🖋

PERSONALIZE

+

VISUALIZE

+

EMOTIONAL(IZE)

=

SELF-AFFIRMATION

Fearless networkers listen 80% and talk 20% of the time because they ask the right questions

Chapter 4

The Dos and Don'ts of Business Networking

"The task we must set for ourselves is not to feel secure, but to be able to tolerate insecurity."

-Erich Fromm

This **Dos** and **Don'ts** segment has suggestions on how to be more assertive at networking. You may be shy or timid! You may avoid reaching out to people. You may be reluctant to greet new people! These tips tell you how to engage others in conversation and develop win-win relationships.

The central focus of the fearless networker rests solely on being a problem solver. Shy and timid networkers do not need the added pressure and anxiety inherent in their thoughts when the focus is on them. When we ask, "What's in it for me? What can I get for my time?" we are under pressure to perform. The appropriate questions are, "How might I help the business owners in attendance? How might I contribute to the professionals attending the event?"

This philosophy of focusing on how you can help and not on what you can get is a mark of the professional networker. You know how to develop and give a self-affirmation talk. Create a talk that will motivate you to be more assertive as a networker.

What to Do at Business Networking Events
1. Have an objective for the number of people you will help at the networking event. Look for ways to meet their needs through your network.
2. Network with those that stand alone at or near the food table or bar. They are easiest to talk to. They are usually shy like yourself!
3. Plan to spend time after the meeting to talk with fellow business people.

4. Look for ways to develop your business relationships. Invite someone for refreshments, breakfast, or lunch or to meet at your office.
5. Listen attentively, after you have asked an open-ended question. Through your network you may be able to meet their needs.
6. Keep your network members at the forefront of your mind.
7. Be observant for people talking openly about their problems.
8. Listen 80% of the time and talk 20% of the time, by asking the right questions.

What Not to Do at Business Networking Events
1. Monopolize the conversation by talking mostly about you and your product or service.
2. Do most of the talking. Ask them open-ended questions. Let the other person do most of the talking. People love to talk about themselves.
3. Stay with those you've come with. It is a good chance you will miss opportunities to network and build relationships.
4. Approach people you know already because you are nervous. The temptation is to stay with the people you recognize and avoid people new to you.
5. Rush into a conversation about what you or a member of your network can do. Continue asking open-ended, probing questions. Show interest in the prospective referral's problems.
6. Be a loner. If you feel uncomfortable, remember to first approach other individuals by themselves. You might see people alone near the drink or buffet tables. They are probably hoping someone will approach them.
7. Be a card dropper, handing out your own business card to each person you come in contact with. Quickly moving on to the next! Leave without making an earnest effort to meet your objective. Be sure that your objective is realistic. Helping one or two people is better than five or six if you are new to networking.
8. Leave without making an earnest effort to meet your objective. Be sure that your objective is realistic. Helping one or two people is better than five or six if you are new to networking.
9. Forget if you are in a referral-sharing group, like BNI. You represent another 20-40 companies not just your company!

Quick Summary: 💡

Have an objective for the number of people you will help at the networking event. Look for ways to meet their needs through your network.

Objectives: 💡

1. To keep your network members at the forefront of your mind.
2. To give yourself a self-affirmation talk just prior to arriving at the business networking event

Action Plan: 💡

1. Develop a self-affirmation talk for the upcoming network event.
2. At the event, talk first with those that are shy just like you.
3. Focus solely on being of service to others.
4. Set reasonable objectives for the number of people you will help. Remember a tiny step may be a big step for you.
5. Keep your network in the forefront of your mind, while listening for needs, issues or concerns.
6. Remember, a big shot (master networker) is just a little shot that kept on shooting.
7. Conduct a $+\triangle$ analysis of what went well and what you could improve or change for the next business-networking event.

Memorizing networking tips, for ease of recall, and following a proven networking tract eases anxiety and stress

Chapter 5

A Proven Networking Tract for Beginners and Professionals
Even the Shy and Timid

"In each of us are heroes; speak to them and they will come forth."

-Anonymous

The following tract is specifically designed for business networking. The tract contains the key elements of successful networking. Taking these steps will ease anxiety and stress that many people experience at networking events. Top-notch business professionals, even accomplished public speakers, can experience networking reluctance. They can be timid when attempting to promote their product or services to others. In other words, we can lack confidence in some areas and be confident in other areas.

This tract will help eliminate the usual anxiety and stress associated with self-promotion. Some discomfort is appropriate. A little adrenaline flowing contributes to a good job at networking. Use the stacking technique, on the next page, to commit these steps of the tract to memory. When committed to memory, you can recall these steps when you are with a prospective referral. Have fun using this tract!

Step 1: Give yourself a personal self-affirmation talk prior to attending a networking event.
Step 2: Keep focused throughout the event on what you can do to help people at the event.
Step 3: Shake hands and introduce yourself.
Step 4: Ask people how they are associated with the host organization.
Step 5: Talk about recent events in the news. Avoid for and against statements.
Step 6: Ask about the type of business & type customers' prospective referrals service.

Step 7: Ask about the challenges with employees, customers, equipment or technology.
Step 8: Listen for specific issues and concerns where your network may be able to assist.
Step 9: Tie the product or service of a network member to the issues and challenges mentioned.
Step 10: Use open-ended questions.
Step 11: Give a 60 seconds introduction of the network member you are recommending.
Step 12: Ask for a meeting between a member of your network, yourself and the referral.
Step 13: Give the referral the network member's business card, as well as your own.
Step 14: Later record dates, time, key issues, challenges and other information in your PDA.
Step 15: Prepare for the next person you want to help. Repeat steps 2-14 above.

Quick Summary: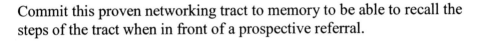

Commit this proven networking tract to memory to be able to recall the steps of the tract when in front of a prospective referral.

Objectives:

1. To utilize this tract in the order presented at all business networking events for next 90 days
2. To commit this tract to memory utilizing the stacking technique

Action Plan:

1. Develop a self-affirmation talk on the use of the networking tract presented in this chapter.
2. Practice the stacking technique until comfortable stating the entire tract in the order presented.
3. Record yourself using a tape player until you are able to say the words in a friendly conversational tone.
4. Use the tract as soon as possible at a networking event. Check with your local Chamber of Commerce for the next business-networking event. Make arrangements to attend.
5. Follow the tract during the networking event.
6. Conduct a $+\triangle$ analysis of what went well while using the tract and what you could have improved or changed for a better result.

Stacking Objects for Mind-Picture:

Rules for stacking technique: Make sure all objects are connected to each other; for example, stuck to, glued to, teetering on, or coming out of. Add bright colors, exaggeration and action to your mind-picture to aid retention. Build stack from bottom to top, #1 is first; #15 is last.

15. Moving van "next"
14. Pen "later-writer"
13. Business card "ABC Network"
12. Calendar
11. Director's Clacker w/ 60 seconds introduction
10. Question marks
 9. Necktie
 8. Ears issues
 7. Challenge flag
 6. Type Business & Type customers' service
 5. Global events (current)
 4. Group association
 3. Handshaking and introduction
 2. Santa's helpers
 1. Self-talk in mirror

Example: Picture this: You are wearing a bright red coat, and you are looking into a spinning MIRROR. Teetering on top of the mirror is a pair of SANTA'S HELPERS wearing bright green elf outfits. Coming out of the bright green elf caps is two SHAKING HANDS. Coming out of the hands are a GROUP of purple STICK FIGURES with their hands raised and balancing a spinning world GLOBE with bright green, yellow and brown colors all around the globe. Glued on the top of the globe and flapping back and forth is an invoice about 3 feet tall with the words MOORE BUSINESS FORMS printed in bright red. Teetering on top of the Moore Business Form is a solid bright pink office door with a gold sign that reads CUSTOMER SERVICE. Coming out of the right top portion of the pink door with the gold customer service sign is a 6-foot tall white flag on a pole with the words CHALLENGE printed in red. Stuck to the top of the CHALLENGE flagpole are two 3 foot tall pink throbbing human EARS. Coming out of the left 3 foot tall pink throbbing ear and sticking straight up is a red, white and blue 6-foot long NECKTIE. Stuck on top of the necktie are two 10 foot tall bright red QUESTION MARKS. Stuck to the top of the QUESTION MARKS is a 4-foot tall all white DIRECTOR'S SCENE CLACKER with the words 60 SECONDS printed in lime green letters. Teetering on top of the director's scene clapper is a spinning 6-foot in diameter bright green CALENDAR. Coming out of the middle of the calendar is a 2-foot tall BUSINESS CARD with the words ABC NETWORK printed in yellow letters. Glued to the top of the business card is a 3 foot tall bright orange ink PEN standing straight up with the words LATER-WRITER printed in a bright pink color. Teetering on top of the ink pen is a 24-foot MOVING VAN with the word NEXT printed in 6-foot tall red letters across the side of the van.

Chapter 6

Five Simple Steps on the Road to Becoming a Fearless Networker

"Before we can make friends with anyone else, we must first make friends with ourselves."

-Eleanor Roosevelt

The Only Tract You Must Master 💡

After building rapport with a prospective referral follow this tract to a tee. The most important key to master networking is active listening. We don't need to be glib or a fast talker to become a champion salesperson or networker. In fact, the opposite is true. We need to ask the right questions, be silent and listen actively for expressed needs. Then we can tie the needs to the product or service of a member of our network. Consistently follow this five-step tract, and you will be well on the road to becoming a fearless networker. Here is an easy way to memorize the tract: using **A.L.T.E.R.**

> **A.**   Asking the right questions
> Need-gathering questions are:
> - Who
> - What
> - When
> - Where
> - Why
> - How
>
> Turn wants into needs by asking clarifying questions. For example, a person says they want an accountant. Through further questioning, you find the real need is for someone to enter financial records into quick books®; for example, a bookkeeper or data entry person. Now you have more information. You know that an accountant or CPA in your

network could help this person find a bookkeeper or data entry person.

Don't focus on the first need, issue or concern and offer a solution. Be patient and keep asking questions. You may get, for example, five needs, issues or concerns. Have the prospective referral prioritize them. Ask, "Which of the five keeps you up at night?" Then listen! A prescription without diagnosis is malpractice!

L. Listening for the Prospective Referrals' Needs
A fearless networker actively listens for needs. Listening with genuine interest shows respect for the prospective referral. Categories of needs could be:
- Employee issues
- Customer issues
- Management issues
- Bottom-line issues
- Process issues

T. Tie the prospective referral's needs to a member of your network's product or service.
- Give prospective referral information on who can help.
- Be a go-giver.

E. Exchange business cards of a member of your network to set an appointment.

R. Reverse card and write the date and time of appointment. Highlight in key words the issues, needs and concerns expressed in the first step. Do this as soon as possible after leaving. This is a good practice even if you have entered the information in your Personal Digital Assistant (PDA) or manual calendar.

Note: Traditional selling had the salesperson spending 10% of the time building rapport, 20% identifying needs, 30% product presentation and 40% closing. Today building relationships require that we spend 90% of our time in discovery (building rapport, finding common interests and identifying needs) with 5% in presentation and gaining commitment respectively. Fearless networking is all about helping others first.

Quick Summary: 💡

Fearless networkers understand how listening and questioning are intertwined. They ask relevant questions. They separate wants from needs and turn wants into needs by asking the right questions.

Objectives: 💡

1. To practice active listening on a daily basis
2. To identify needs by asking penetrating questions: who, what, when, where, why and how
3. To tie needs identified to network member's product or service
4. To turn wants into needs through asking further clarifying questions
5. To learn the **P.L.I.E.R.S.** tract (See Chapter 14) and the **A.L.T.E.R.** track to be able to provide hot referrals to your network

Action Plan: 💡

1. Prepare to follow this tract in a real world environment by first giving yourself a self-affirmation talk.
2. Focus on making a contribution. Ask, "How can I contribute to this networking event or meeting?"
3. Remember to begin with small talk prior to using the five simple steps toward becoming a fearless networker.
4. Follow the 5 simple steps in the order presented in this chapter.
5. After the networking event or meeting, conduct a $+\triangle$ analysis of what went well. Determine what you could have improved or changed in using the 5 simple steps for a better result.

Chapter 7

Attitudes of Fearless Networkers

"What lies before us and what lies behind us are small matters compared to what lies within. And when we bring what lies within us out into the world miracles happen."

-Henry David Thoreau

Fearless networkers are separated from mediocre networkers by six inches between their ears – their attitudes! The good news is that mediocre networkers can become fearless networkers. Master networkers are not born. In most cases, they were once shy networkers! Read these ten attitudes of fearless networkers. Notice the powerful words and that they express commitment, belief and conviction:

Attitudes that Express Commitment, Belief and Conviction

Fearless networkers:

1. Have a genuine desire and willingness to help others grow their business
2. Are committed to being "go-givers"
3. Choose to believe that they can and will make a contribution to any networking situation
4. Take action rather than let fear compromise their drive to serve others
5. Constantly, conscientiously and consistently utilize the power of self-affirmation talks using visualization (See Chapter 3)
6. Have an unwavering belief in the universal law of reciprocity, (give and you will receive)

7. Show a keen interest in the other person's business and personal needs
8. Understand that fearless networking is less about being a "go-getter" and more about being a "go-giver"
9. Are committed to leading a life of service as evidenced by their involvement in the community
10. Do not let negativity, criticism and envy deter them from giving and serving

Quick Summary: 💡

They have a genuine desire and willingness to help others grow their business. They consistently demonstrate this by providing referrals to members of their network.

Objectives: 💡

1. To develop a habit of focusing less on my needs and more on the needs of others
2. To review and reflect on the universal law of reciprocity; give and you will receive

Action Plan: 💡

1. Review and reflect on the joy of service, "My Philosophy of Networking."
2. Make a habit of utilizing the "Fearless Networker's Interview Checklist." Strive to answer "yes" to all questions.
3. Review and reflect on the ten attitudes of fearless networkers before every networking situation.
4. After a networking situation, conduct a +△ analysis using the ten attitudes of fearless networkers. Ascertain what went well and what attitudes and behaviors you could have used to improve your performance for a better result.

MEMORY BOOSTER

Fearless Networkers have a **C.A.R.I.N.G** Attitude:

Choose to believe they can contribute to any networking situation

Act on their desire to serve

Respond to negativity and criticism by continuing to give and serve

Intently interested in their networks' business and personal needs

Nurtures relationships

Go-give is first priority rather than go-get

Fearless networkers demonstrate genuine interest and caring, building solid relationships as a result.

Chapter 8

Behaviors of Fearless Networkers

*"If you want a response, you have
to ask for it."*
-John Huenefeld

Fearless networkers are daring, bold, courageous and confident. They are willing to do the things that others won't, so that they can reap rewards abundantly while others are saying, "I can't." Read these ten behavioral traits of fearless networkers. Memorize them. Take action and reap the rewards of behaving selflessly. Notice the action-oriented nature of these behaviors and how well they complement the attitudes of fearless networkers covered in the previous chapter.

Behaviors of Fearless Networkers:

1. Flexible and adaptable to change
2. Prepare and use well-planned pre-qualifying questions
3. Risk-taking (risk rejection, risk giving referrals without guarantees of getting referrals back in return, risk criticism)
4. Take Action on their plans (goals, objectives, self-improvement)
5. Confronts with care (never pushy, argumentative or over-aggressive)
6. Actively listens for issues, concerns, needs
7. Go-givers (constantly seeking referrals for others in network and a willingness to give of their time to help or mentor others)
8. Tactfully remind members of your network who are receiving referrals from you how best to market your services to their network (never blatantly ask for a referral in return)
9. Conducts regular self-check ups (evaluations) (looks for lessons to be learned from each encounter with a prospective referral)
10. Is active in the community (giving back)

Stacking Objects for Mind-Picture:

Rules for stacking technique: Make sure all objects are connected to each other; for example, stuck to, glued to, teetering on or coming out of. Add bright colors, exaggeration and action to your mind-picture to aid retention. Build stack from bottom to top, #1 is first; #10 is last.

> 10. Community action
> 9. Self-check ups
> 8. Tacks in mind
> 7. Go-Giver's T-shirt
> 6. Throbbing Ears
> 5. Car fronts (grilles) CARE wreath
> 4. Action on plans
> 3. Risk-taking
> 2. Prepares questions
> 1. Change agent

Example: Picture this: You are a ticket agent and you are dropping gold and silver coins (CHANGE) that are dancing on floor. Coming out of the top of one of the dancing coins is a ten foot tall green PEAR with a three foot tall QUESTION MARK glued on top of the pear. Stuck on top of the question mark is a wrist watch with the word RISK in red letters printed on a white watch face. Teetering on top of the watch is an AIRPLANE with an ACTION figure wearing army fatigues resembling you and dancing on top of the plane. Stuck on top of the action figure's head is a CAR FRONT (grille) with a wreath stuck on the front with a white satin ribbon with the word CARE in red letters. Coming out of the top of the car front (grille) is a six-foot tall pink throbbing EAR. Glued on top of the pink throbbing ear is you wearing a full body length red T-shirt with the words GO-GIVER'S in white letters. Stuck on top of your head is a plastic model of a brain (mind) filled with gold TACKS. Teetering on top of the plastic brain is you with a two foot tall MIRROR encased in white plastic in your right hand and you are CHECKING for blemishes while holding the mirror UP. Coming out of the mirror is a red conference room door with the words COMMUNITY ACTION Committee Meeting in bright yellow letters.

Quick Summary:

Commit this proven track to memory and review, on a weekly basis, how well you are behaving as a fearless networker for a period of 90 days or until behaving, as a fearless networker is a habit.

Objectives:

1. To utilize all or a large portion of this tract in the order presented each week for next 90 days
2. To commit this tract to memory utilizing the stacking technique

Action Plan:

1. Develop a self-affirmation talk on the use of the networking tract presented in this chapter.
2. Practice the stacking technique until comfortable stating the entire tract in the order presented.
3. Conduct a +△ analysis of what went well while using the Behavior's of Fearless Networkers tract and what you could have improved or changed for a better result.

Chapter 9

Networking Is Easiest When You Are Being Observant

"We can choose to create of our lives an accident or an adventure."

-Anonymous

Have fun with this simple, yet powerful approach.

Recently, I was waiting on AAA towing service at a building where one of my clients resides. I saw a woman who appeared to be in distress. I asked, "Can I help?"

She was pounding on the door of an office. She said, "Do you know the man who offices here? I have a 2:00pm appointment with him."

I said, "No. I don't." I noticed that the door sign read "Private Investigator." I said, "Maybe he will be here in a few minutes. He could have gotten stuck in traffic." This didn't seem to offer very much hope. She continued to pace back and forth. I asked her, "Did you try the side door to the office?"

She said, "Yes." Someone came walking toward us. "May I use your phone in your office?" The woman nodded okay, and we followed her into a mortgage office. I overheard the woman in distress telling the person she was speaking with, "I have an appointment with a private investigator, and he did not show up for the appointment." In a hushed tone, she said, "I am not at a place where I can speak freely and discuss the matter." She glanced back at me. Reluctantly she said, "My husband left town with the money." A few more words were spoken and she hung up.

As she was leaving, I said, "I apologize. I could not help but overhear that you are in need of a private investigator." She nodded in the affirmative. I introduced myself. "I belong to a business networking group, and we have a private investigator in the group. He is professional and knowledgeable. I have his card right here in my card file." After finding Bill's business card, I said, "Bill Pellerin of Texas Investigative Services will have someone you can speak with about your need. So please call him. I am certain that you will be pleased with his service."

When I finally got back to my office an hour later, after waiting another 30 minutes for AAA, I had a voice mail message from Bill Pellerin of Texas Investigative Services. "Ken, thanks for the referral. We have already been able to help the person you referred."

This story illustrates how easy it is to network when you are observant. Look for people in need. Ask the right questions to determine the need. Keep the phrase, "How can I help?" in the forefront of your mind.

Follow these seven suggestions to network anywhere:

1. Reach out and greet anywhere!
2. Engage and tune-in to conversations going on around you.
3. Look for people in distress and introduce yourself.
4. Ask, "Can I be of assistance?" If so, show genuine compassion and speak in a caring, conversational way.
5. Think of who in your network could be of assistance.
6. Exchange business cards.

Quick Summary:

Meet and greet people anywhere. Be observant for signs of distress, frustration or worry. Take action and ask if you can be of assistance.

Objectives:

1. To be observant and sensitive for people in need
2. To be attuned to body language and tone of voice to recognize people in need
3. To keep your network in the forefront of your mind
4. To have your business card file holder available at all times

Action Plan:

1. Develop and use a self-affirmation talk prior to using these steps.
2. Be observant for people in distress when visiting office buildings, post offices, etc.
3. Be eager to assist without being pushy or overly aggressive.
4. Offer the services of someone in your network.
5. Conduct a $+\triangle$ analysis of how well you used these steps, what steps you
    could have improved or changed for a better result.

Join a networking group and practice your 60 seconds presentation weekly. When presenting your presentation, make sure that you are excited about it and eager to share it. Remember, enthusiasm sells!

Chapter 10

Developing Your 60 Seconds Product or Service Presentation

*"I don't know what your destiny will
be, but one thing I know; the only ones among you
who will be really happy are those who will have
sought and found how to serve."*

-Albert Schweitzer

In my networking group, we have an opportunity to give a 60 seconds product or service presentation. Importantly, we are providing our network, some 30 marketers of our product or service, vital information. Thus, people other than us are inspired to share accurate and positive information to prospective referrals in their circle of influence. One of my assignments, as Educational Coordinator for my networking group, was to help our members shine when they present their 60 seconds product or service presentation.

A word about 30 seconds elevator speeches:

Those who want to develop a shorter version, which takes about 30 seconds, keep the faith. This "elevator speech" is about the time we have between floors in an elevator. Once we have developed a 60 seconds presentation, we can easily scale back our 60 seconds presentations to 30 seconds. Practice being concise and to the point! All the information you will need for your 30 seconds elevator speech is already in your 60 seconds product or service presentations.

Author's Note: The best time to gently prod for a referral is doing your 60 seconds presentation, followed by your "dance" meeting (See Chapter 20.) Remember to state specifically the best referral for you. Avoid the phrase "Do you know anyone..." it's far too vague! See example below of the phrase "I'm Specifically Looking For":

Elements of the 60 Seconds Product or Service Presentation:
Name: First and Last:

Name of Company:

Type of Business:

Key Products or Services:

Ideal Customer:

I'm Specifically Looking For:

Benefits to Customers for Having or Owning my Product or Service:

Awards or Recognition:

What Inspires Me about my Product or Service:

What Makes Us Unique from our Competition:

Developing my "Hook" or "Catchy Phrase":

Example:

This is a presentation developed for the founder of my networking group, Daisy Morales, in Houston, Texas:

Name: First and Last: Daisy Morales
Name of Company: Coldwell Banker United, Realtors
Type of Company: Residential Real Estate
Key Products or Services: Buying and Selling Homes, MLS, Internet (Calculations and Photos), Price Comparisons, Relocation Assistance
Ideal Customer: First Time Buyers, Families "Moving Up," Someone who appreciates the value of a realtor, anyone looking to "Buy" or "Sell" or "Relocate."
I'm Specifically Looking For: Apartment dwellers complaining about the lack of privacy living in apartment complexes or a zero equity position.

Benefits to a Customer for Having or Owning our Product or Service:

- We're Totally Committed to Going the "Extra Mile."
- We Get Very High Marks for Customer Service.
- We Assist You in Truly Understanding the Value of the Home You're Buying or Selling.

What Inspires Me About my Product or Service? What Makes Us Unique from our Competition?
- We Work Hard to Please Our Customers.
- We Truly Provide Excellent Service.
- "Pride of Ownership" is not a Buzz Phrase.
- We Help Find Your Dream Home.

Awards and Recognition: Rookie of the Year, Customer Rating (4.86 out of 5.0)

Developing my "Hook" or Catchy Phrase" and Using Key Phrases:
- Key Phrases:
  - Customer Satisfaction Is Key
  - Find Your Dream Home
  - Totally Committed
  - Understand True Value of Real Estate
  "Catchy Phrases," "Hooks" or "Adages"
  "At Coldwell Banker, We Don't Just Give You a House Key: To Us Your Total Satisfaction is the Key to Your House."
  "At Coldwell Banker, we make dream homes a reality."
  "Have you heard of the chicken and pig story? Well, to some of our competitors, service is like a chicken providing eggs. It is all in a days work! At Coldwell Banker, we are like the pig providing bacon. To us, service is a total commitment!"
  "At Coldwell Banker, we don't just find the home you love. We find the home you fall 'in love' with."

Developing a 60 seconds Product or Service Presentation Worksheet:

Name: First and Last:
Name of Company:
Type of Business:
Key Products and Services (top 3-5):
Ideal Customer:
I'm Specifically Looking For: (Narrow down to a best type referral)
Benefits for Customers Having or Owning my Products and Services (top 3-5):
What Inspires Me about my Product or Service? What Makes Us Unique from our Competition?
Awards and Recognition:
Developing my "Catch Phrase" or "Hook" (Use key phrases from benefits and inspires section.):
"Hooks" or "Catchy Phrases":

Tip: To deliver a 30 seconds "commercial," give your name, company name, type-company, key products and services, ideal customer, what makes you unique and your hook! (Some recommend beginning with your hook)

Quick Summary:

In developing your 60 seconds product or service presentations, think of the features and benefits that excite you! Build your presentation around that information.

Objectives:

1. To develop a winning 60 seconds product or service presentation
2. To focus on what makes your product or service unique
3. To be specific in describing your best type referral (may vary occasionally depending on product or service focus)

Action Plan:

1. Use the worksheet provided to develop your 60 seconds product or service presentation.
2. Practice your presentation using a tape player. Remember, it is not only what you say but how you say it.
3. If you have access to a camcorder, use it to videotape your presentation. You will see how you come across, mannerisms and voice tone.
4. Based on the video review, make improvements in your presentation style.
5. After several practice sessions conduct a $+\triangle$ analysis to ascertain what you did well in your presentation and what you could improve or change for a better result.

Chapter 11

Marsh Mantras
Words to Build a Network – and a Life

"It doesn't matter what we do until we accept ourselves. Once we accept ourselves it doesn't matter what we do."

-Anonymous

Giving and servicing provides joy and satisfaction when we network from the heart and not the head. Stress and anxiety are reduced when we stop focusing on ourselves and focus on helping others. Also, read other books on this topic. Understand the power and rewards of unselfish networking. In fact, while reading Harvey Mackay's book *"Dig Your Well Before You're Thirsty,"* I came across Mackay Maxims. I was inspired to write and share with you my own versions.

Marsh Mantras! Words to Build a Network – and Life

- Your reputation is your most valuable possession. It is your biggest asset for successful networking.
- The #1 way to reduce fear of networking is to change your focus from what I can get to what I can give.
- Before any networking function, plan the number of connections you will make for people in your network.
- Being a go-giver is more conducive to building long-term relationships than being a go-getter.
- Go out on a limb, that's where the fruit is!
- One of the best ways to reduce stress about your livelihood is to focus on helping some people enhance their livelihood.

- One truth about life is that life keeps giving us the same lessons until we learn them. Once we learn a lesson, life presents us with our next challenge (lesson to be learned).
- If you're in a referral-sharing group, only to get referrals, you're in the wrong group. Ivan Misner, Business Network International, Founder & CEO, says, "Givers Gain!"
- People do business with people they know and like. They will continue to do business when they grow to trust and respect you.
- The best listeners make the best networkers. When you respond to a prospective referral's need through listening and provide a solution through someone from your network, you become a powerful ally.
- Have a positive expectancy that the referrals you give will provide you with many blessings.
- Have no expectation about what you will receive in return. Your blessings could come in another area where it's needed just as much. The Universal Law of Reciprocity, a Biblical principle, is as real as the law of gravity!

Quick Summary:

The Marsh Mantras are words to build a network and life. Review and reflect on them often, especially if business networking is not working for you.

Objectives:

1. To review Marsh Mantras when you want to be inspired before attending a networking event or meeting
2. To review Marsh Mantras when you're feeling down about the lack of referrals you are giving to your network

Action Plan:

1. Read Marsh Mantras prior to attending an event.
2. From your reading, select 2 or 3 mantras to reflect on as you are pre-planning the number of connections you will make at the networking event.
3. Use Marsh Mantras to help you conduct your $+\triangle$ analysis after the networking event. Ascertain what went well and what you could improve or change for better results.

People aren't strangers if you've already met them. The trick is to meet them before you need their help.

-- Harvey Mackay

The 10 Commandments of Fearless Networking!

"Networking is not a numbers game. The idea is not to see how many people you can meet. The idea is to compile a list of people you can count on."

-Harvey Mackay

THE TEN COMMANDMENTS OF FEARLESS NETWORKING FROM THE "NEWER TESTAMENT"

1. **Thou shall listen 80% of the time and talk 20% of the time**
(Listening with your heart shows respect, caring and courtesy for the prospective referral. True listening is, wanting to hear)

2. **Thou shall think about what you can contribute rather than what you can get when attending networking functions**
(Thinking of how you can help others feel good about themselves instead of thinking about how you can get others to feel good about you, is the hall mark of a fearless networker)

3. **Thou shall keep your network in the forefront of your mind**
(When in front of a prospective referral you are always ready to recommend a member of your network when you can not personally help)

4. **Thou shall follow up and follow through**
(Don't make promises you can't keep; but, keep the promises you make)

5. **Thou shall spend 90% of face time building relationships**
(I spend 90% of my time in rapport building, identifying common interests, needs identification and 5% on my own presentation and 5% on my close)

6. **Thou shall adhere to the law of reciprocity**
(Learning how to give with no expectations and learning how to receive without guilt or embarrassment)

7. **Thou shall strive to give only pre-qualified "hot" referrals**
(Giving "hot" referrals motivates you to want to provide more "hot" referrals)

8. **Thou shall not rush into a conversation about your product**
(First, show interest in the prospective referral's dreams, goals, issues and concerns. It takes time to build trust; the linchpin of effective relationships)

9. **Thou shall stay in contact with referrals given to you**
(Nurturing through phone calls, cards and e-mails helps build relationships)

10. **Thou shall teach your clients and referrals to know how to generate referrals for you**
(You must be specific in describing your best prospect and in how to approach the prospect)

Quick Summary: 💡

Consistently think about how you can help or contribute to a prospective referral's business.

Objective: 💡

1. To review "The 10 Commandments of Fearless Networking" prior to networking for inspiration.

Action Plan: 💡

1. Review and reflect on "The 10 Commandments of Fearless Networking" prior to attending a networking event or meeting.
2. Select three of the 10 commandments to focus on during a networking function.
3. Use the 10 commandments together with Marsh Mantras for review and reflection. Conduct a $+\triangle$ analysis of your performance in light of applying both the mantras and commandments at a networking event, covering what went well and what you could improve or change for a better result.

Chapter 12

Effectively Utilizing Business Cards as a Networking Tool

"The three most powerful words in the English language: just do it!"

-Anonymous

Be prepared! Follow the scouting motto! I delivered this presentation to my networking group to help them use business cards as networking tools. To leave a positive first impression, have your own business cards and your network members, available. Follow these guidelines, and you will make a surefire, positive first impression.

The Right Way to Use Business Cards as Networking Tools

1. At networking events, don't give out business cards immediately upon introducing yourself. This behavior can derail further conversation, other than cursory, polite banter about each other's business. Instead, read the business card you received.
2. Then begin a dialog using three simple steps: (1) Ask the right questions (who, what, when, where, why or how) building rapport and then focusing on needs, issues and concerns (2) Listen to the needs of the individual (3) Tie the needs to the product or service of your fellow networkers. Now, handout your business cards.
3. Jot down highlighted trigger words indicating the needs mentioned by the person you interviewed. Later transfer this information to your manual or electronic database on your PC or Personal Digital Assistant.
4. Immediately after the networking meeting, on the back top half of the business cards received, write the event's name, date, location and who gave you the card.

5. Keep your business cardholder handy for easy access to your fellow network members' business cards.
6. Have pre-written, in red ink, "Thank You!" According to Tom Hopkins, author of *Sales Techniques for Dummies*, your business card will stand out from other business cards. Make your "Gracias" fit the heritage, Spanish, Asian.
7. Always have a sufficient quantity of your business cards with you. Keep at least 20 extra business cards in the glove compartment of your vehicle.
8. Keep several business cards in the side, outer coat pocket of your jacket. Right side if you are right-handed and left side if left-handed. This avoids a frantic search for your business cards.
9. When you hand out a business card, hold it chest high, with face of card facing the prospect. Many people never look at a business card before pocketing it.
10. Make sure all information on your business card is current. If you must make a correction, line out the old information with one straight line. Neatly print the new or updated information.
11. Never use business cards that are printed on too dark or glossy card stock. They can't be written on legibly.
12. Always insert business cards in thank you notes, brochures and proposals.

Quick Summary:

Your business card plays a vital part in making an effective first impression. The cards should be well kempt, with up-to-date information.

Objectives:

1. To avoid handing out your business card right after you introduce yourself
2. To jot down key information on the back of business cards you receive
3. To record information to jog your memory about needs discussed

Action Plan:

1. Prepare yourself for effectively networking using your business cards.
2. First give yourself a self-affirmation talk tailored to the effective use of business cards.
3. Keep sufficient business cards handy. (20 extras in your car)
4. Pre-print the words, "Thank You!" in red ink on your cards.
5. Keep current information (e-mail, fax, voice, cell #'s, address) on your business cards.
6. Conduct a $+\triangle$ analysis on the effective use of your business cards at business networking events. Ascertain what you did well and what you could improve or change for a better result.

One secret is to be other-person focused when you are attempting to make a connection

Chapter 13

My Secret of Giving Lots of "Hot" Referrals

"I'm a great believer in luck, and the
harder I work the more I have of it."

-Thomas Jefferson

The Best of the Best

This chapter on "My Secrets of Giving Lots of 'Hot' Referrals" has the best of best advice in this "how to" manual. 95% of all my referrals are 4 or 5 on the "tepid" to "hot" scale of our networking group's referral slip. 5, is the hottest. 1 is the most tepid. I've given as many as 16 "hot" referrals in one week and so can you. The following are my key reasons for success in this arena:

1. The more referrals you give, the easier it is to generate more referrals.
2. Think about referrals early in the week to give you plenty of time.
3. Giving "hot" referrals increases your joy and satisfaction of helping others grow their businesses. So the only type of referrals you desire to give are "hot" referrals
4. Challenge yourself and set your referral goals high.
5. Become other-person focused when you are with clients, business associates and contacts.
6. When you "dance" or meet with others to learn about their businesses, think of people who might need their products and services. Dancing, I believe, is my number one success step. After every "dance," I usually have one or more referrals to give my "dance" partner. (For a detailed explanation of the "dance" concept, see Chapter 20.)
7. Become good at asking penetrating questions, who, what, when, where, why or how, to ascertain needs, issues and concerns.

8. Master the **A.L.T.E.R.** tract (See Chapter 6) and become proficient in the use of the **P.L.I.E.R.S.** tract (See Chapter 14).
9. Keep probing for needs, issues, concerns and priorities, and you will provide a better pre-qualified and prepared referral. Probing can also lead to finding the best person that can help the prospective referral.
10. **Don't Wait! Interrogate!** You might be too late to get the referral or the business. This **DWI** you can be proud of!

Quick Summary: 💡

The more referrals given, the easier it is to generate more referrals. When in front of a prospective referral use the **DWI** approach to elicit more need-based information. Become proficient at using the **A.L.T.E.R.** tract and the **P.L.I.E.R.S.** tract.

Objectives: 💡

1. To review and reflect on the success principles of giving "Hot" referrals
3. To focus on helping your fellow network members
4. To conduct a $+\triangle$ analysis to ascertain what went well when you followed the success secrets
5. To determine what to do to improve or change to get a better result

Action Plan: 💡
1. Gradually increase the number of referrals you give to members of your network.
2. Review and reflect on these success principles at the beginning of the workweek.
3. Become more other-person focused.
4. Conduct a $+\triangle$ analysis at the end of the workweek. Ascertain what went well in your efforts to give more "hot" referrals and what could improve or change for a better result.

MEMORY BOOSTER

5 Success Secrets of a Referral-Giving CHAMP:

Challenge yourself. Set your referral goals high.

Have "Hot" referrals to give 95% or more of the time

Ask penetrating questions -- who, what, when, where, why and how

Maintain an active "dance" schedule (See chapter 20).

Provide pre-qualified referrals only! Use both the **A.L.T.E.R.** and **P.L.I.E.R.S.** tracts.

The number one key to the success of fearless networkers is consistently providing pre-qualified referrals!

Chapter 14

Pre-Qualifying Your Referrals

"A prescription without diagnosis is malpractice."

-Author Unknown

Providing solid pre-qualified referrals (following the **A.L.T.E.R.** tract (See Chapter 6) and this Chapter's **P.L.I.E.R.S.** tract) is the most important help you can give members of your network. Asking the following questions will help qualify your referrals in three categories. (1) Do your prospects need what members of your network have to offer? (2) Are your prospects the decision makers? (3) What are the levels of interest of your prospects? Remember: Build rapport and use the **A.L.T.E.R.** tract first before using this tract.

The best tool for the job is **P.L.I.E.R.S.!** Here is an easy way to remember **P.L.I.E.R.S.:**

Acronym:

P = Presently: What does the prospective referral have *presently?*

L = Like: What does the prospective referral *like* about what they have now?

I = Improve: What would the prospective referral like to *improve* about what they have now? Note: in a study conducted by Dr. Frederick Reichheld and reported in the Harvard Business Review, 66% or more of customers who chose a new supplier said they were satisfied with their former supplier.

E = End-Decision: Who will be making the *end* or final *decision* on the purchase?

R = Resolve: What would it mean to the prospective referral if a member of my network can *resolve* the challenge or issue and significantly improve what the prospective referral has presently? Note: In a study conducted by Dr. Robert Peterson of the University of Texas, 85% of customers who said they were satisfied with the service of their current supplier were willing to try other suppliers.

S = Set Up Meeting: When would be a good time for a member of my network to call on the decision-makers, face-to-face or over the phone?

The following example involves a member of my TEC Associates Round Table (T.A.R.T.). For more on T.A.R.T., see Chapter 1 "My Philosophy of Networking."

Example:

Referring T.A.R.T. member: Ms. Jones, what type of retirement or benefit plan do you have <u>presently</u> for your employees?

Prospective Referral: We are currently considering establishing a 401k plan and modifying our incentive-based compensation plan.

Referring T.A.R.T. member: What do you <u>like</u> about your current compensation plan?

Prospective Referral: The plan has helped to motivate employees to meet performance standards important to the growth of our company.

Referring T.A.R.T. member: What would you like to <u>improve</u> about your current compensation plan?

Prospective Referral: Our current plan does not offer retirement-type compensation tied to the profitability of the company.

Consequently, some of our competitors have convinced some of our best employees to join their companies by offering a 401k or retirement-type package. To keep ahead of the competition, we will need to do the same.

Referring T.A.R.T. member: Who besides you will be making the end (final) decision on the type of retirement plan your company selects?

Prospective Referral: It will be our Chief Financial Officer and me.

Referring T.A.R.T. member: What would it mean to you and your company, if one of my associates can resolve your compensation/retirement dilemma? The plan would impress your employees and have a positive impact on your company's bottom-line.

Prospective Referral: That would be great! Who is this person?

Referring T.A.R.T. member: My associate's name is David Trifon, LPL Branch Manager with Koinonia Financial in The Woodlands, Texas. He has a sincere, caring connection with employees. He helps them see the direct benefits for being a part of the plan chosen. When would be a good time next week for David and me to meet with you and your CFO? Let's give David several dates and times. I'll get back with you to set up a meeting date and time convenient with all parties.

Referring T.A.R.T. member: You will be very impressed with David. He sincerely cares about his clients. He is committed to making sure they understand the plan chosen and are satisfied with the product and his service. David is excellent on follow through on what he promises. Periodically he follows up to inform you on the status of your chosen plan.

Quick Summary:

The most important help you can give a member of your network is to provide a pre-qualified referral.

Objectives:

1. To use proven on-target pre-qualifying questions when face-to-face with a prospective referral
2. To provide solid pre-qualified referrals to my network

Action Plan:

1. Practice the **P.L.I.E.R.S.** tract until comfortable with it and it sounds conversational in tone.
2. Combine the **P.L.I.E.R.S.** tract with the **A.L.T.E.R.** tract (See Chapter 6) to provide a pre-qualified hot referral
3. Use a tape player in your practice to help with this.
4. Give yourself a self-affirmation talk prior to using the tract in a real-world situation.
5. Conduct a $+\triangle$ analysis to ascertain what went well and what steps of the **P.L.I.E.R.S.** tract you could change your performance for a better result.

Chapter 15

Top Ten Mistakes of Business Networking

"Success is 90% starting and 10% not stopping."
-A.D. Kessler

Following is a list of what I believe are the top ten mistakes of business networking. Each mistake has its own serious consequence. For example, consider Mistake #4: "Not pre-qualifying a referral *before* you give it to a member of your network or giving a tepid referral." The outcome is that the Universal Law of Reciprocity, give and you will receive, applies in this situation. Therefore, it's no coincidence that the reason you are receiving "tepid" referrals is because you are giving "tepid" referrals!

Mistake #1: You do not follow up on referrals you are given in a timely fashion.

Result #1: You might not receive another referral from this person. The person desiring your service or product could judge this as lack of professionalism on your part or how you treat your customers.

Mistake #2: You expect a lead from the person you are giving a referral to.

Result #2: Even if you've asked for a referral, don't expect one in return. Unfulfilled expectations can lead to disenchantment with the referral-sharing process. Instead, trust the Law of Reciprocity!

Mistake #3: You exhibit poor active listening skills.

Result #3: Failure to listen for needs results in missed opportunities to give "hot" pre-qualified referrals.

Mistake #4: You do not pre-qualify a referral before you give it to your network member.

Result #4: You are not a true networker! The referrals you receive from your network may not be pre-qualified. So don't be surprised.

Mistake #5: You do not have enough business cards available for a networking event or meeting.

Result #5: You will have regrets! Your reputation as a networker will be sullied. It is never okay to shrug it off in a lighthearted manner.

Mistake #6: You do not keep network member advised of the status of the referral.

Result #6: This is disrespectful and could lead to poor relations with individual.

Mistake #7: You only think about your business when in front of a prospect or client.

Result#7: You will lose the opportunity to be a member of a "Givers Gain" group. You may end up the only person growing your business.

Mistake #8: You have poor probing skills and fail to ask penetrating questions.

Result #8: Your referrals will lack needs, issues and challenges of the referral. Your network members will essentially be making a cold call.

Mistake #9: You do not know how to ask for referrals or you're not specific enough in your asking

Result #9: Your request will be too vague. For example: "Do you know anyone…" Consequently, you are getting only a few referrals, if any.

Mistake #10: You have a "what's in it for me" attitude instead of a "how can I help" attitude.

Result #10: Stress, anxiety, neediness and pressure will rule your day.

Quick Summary: 💡

Making these top ten mistakes can result in serious consequences. You will be a poor performer as a networker.

Objectives: 💡

1. To avoid making these top ten mistakes; thus avoiding the costly outcomes
2. To review and reflect on the top ten mistakes at least once a month

Action Plan: 💡

1. After each networking event, reflect on the top ten mistakes to see if you have inadvertently violated these suggestions.
2. Commit to focusing on achieving the positive, profitable results.
3. Strive to rectify any mistakes. Conduct a $+\triangle$ analysis to ascertain what you did well in your attempt to reform and what could you improve.

MEMORY BOOSTER:

Avoid making an **E.P.I.C.** mistake:

Expecting a referral in return for one given

Poor pre-qualifying skills (listening, questioning/probing)

Interested primarily in receiving referrals

Choosing to think only about your business when in front of a prospect

Not getting referrals? Perhaps, you're not being specific enough when describing your ideal prospect

Chapter 16

How to Excel at Getting "Hot" Referrals to Come to You

"Success is sweet, but usually has a scent of sweat about it."

-Anonymous

If this is the first Chapter you are reading in this book, stop! I strongly urge you to go back and read the first 3 Chapters. This book is primarily about giving, not getting! Building relationships through Fearless Networking works when you understand and practice the Universal Law of Reciprocity, "give and you will receive." Beginning with this Chapter of the book will hamper your efforts at building sustainable win-win relationships. Building relationships require being other-person focused.

Success Tip #1:
Self-direct yourself each day. Visualize people who you can help. Affirm that you will support your fellow BNI members and help grow their businesses. Visualize yourself, confidently asking for prospective referrals from members of your network. (See Chapter 3.)

Success Tip #2:
Be very specific in your request. The phrase "Do you know anyone who..." is too general and vague. Help your network member help you by having her to identify a circle of influence group. The better question would then be "Do you know anyone in your professional women's group, at your job or in your family who...?"

Success Tip #3:
"Dance" or meet with your fellow network members and describe your most profitable prospective client. (See the "Dance Information Sheet" in Chapter 20.) Follow the system identified in the chapter and teach your network members to market your product or service through "word of mouth."

Success Tip #4:
The best time to ask for a referral is in your 60 seconds presentation. Identify your ideal client but also state the type referral you are specifically looking for, to approach about your product or service. Just saying my ideal client is the small business owner is not specific enough! For example, let's say you are a 401k Specialist and you are asking a member of your network to refer you to small business owners. You would help your network member help you by saying, "Do you know anyone in your Chamber CEO round table that has raised an issue about their 401k program? I am specifically looking for a small business owner considering offering a 401k type program or is having trouble supporting one."

Success Tip #5:
Help your network members to know how to pre-qualify a prospective referral for you. "Dance" or meet with them and practice the **A.L.T.E.R.** and **P.L.I.E.R.S.** tracts (Chapter 6 and 14 respectively) using your product or service and the product or service of your network member. If you consider the other 20, 30 or 40 members of your networking group your marketing team. You must train them to market your product!

Success Tip #6:
Tell your network members to fight the impulse to offer a solution by jumping on the first need, issue or concern mentioned. Instead implore them to continue to ask open-ended questions until the prospective referral has given several needs, issues or concerns. Then have their prospective referral prioritize the needs, issues or concerns.

Success Tip #7:
When you give a referral to a member of your network never directly ask for one or expect one in return. This approach puts pressure on your network member and actually impedes her efforts in clearly thinking of a prospective referral for you. Instead use a gentle prod approach by saying, "now here's how you may be able to help me in the future." This may be a good time to bring out a "Dance Information Sheet" if you haven't used one in a previous "dance" or meeting with the network member.

Success Tip #8:
Tell your network member, even if the prospective referral emphatically says, "Have your associate contact call me," to continue pre-qualifying the referral. Have your network member tell the prospective referral the reason he is asking more questions is that he wants to clearly explain the needs, issues or concerns identified so that his associate (you) would know how to best help.

Quick Summary: 💡

The chances of receiving a solid referral, is slim to none if you are not being specific enough when identifying your prospective referral. Simply saying, my ideal customer is the small business owner, is not good enough!

Objectives: 💡

1. To use the proven success tips recorded in this chapter
2. To be specific when asking for a referral
3. To let the Universal Law of Reciprocity work by helping your network members help you. By stating specifically what you looking for.

Action Plan: 💡

1. Be specific in your 60 seconds presentation in describing your ideal prospect
2. Teach your network member how to pre-qualify a prospective referral for you, using the **A.L.T.E.R.** and **P.L.I.E.R.S.** tracts in this book.
4. Purchase a copy of Fearless Networking for key network members.
5. Buying this book for your key network members to learn how to market your product or service through the best form of advertising "word of mouth" is definitely worth the investment, don't you agree?
6. Conduct a $+\triangle$ analysis on what's working well in receiving "hot" referrals. Follow the success tips recorded in this chapter. Then determine what could you improve or change to be more effective at getting "hot" referrals to come to you.

Chapter 17

Paradoxical Commandments of Fearless Networking

"Keep away from people who try to belittle your ambitions. Small people always do that, but really great people make you feel that you, too, can become great."

-Mark Twain

Many years ago someone gave me a copy of the "Paradoxical Commandments of Leadership," (PCL) author unknown. I decided to consider them from a fearless networker perspective.

"Words of Wisdom in Summary"

1. Some people are unfair, unreasonable and self-centered when it comes to sharing referrals.
   Give them referrals anyway.
2. If you do a good job giving lots of referrals, some people will accuse you of selfish ulterior motives.
   Do good anyway.
3. If you are successful, as a fearless networker, sometimes you win false friends and true enemies.
   Succeed anyway.
4. The good you do today, in giving referrals, will be forgotten tomorrow.
   Do good anyway.
5. Honesty and frankness can sometimes make you vulnerable.
   Be honest and frank anyway.

85

6. Sometimes the fearless networkers with the biggest ideas can be shot down by the so-so networkers with the smallest ideas.
   Think big anyway.
7. Most people favor underdogs but follow only top dogs.
   Fight for a few underdogs anyway.
8. You may spend years building your network and it may be destroyed overnight.
   Build anyway.
9. Some people will wait, watch and expect referrals but never have any to give.
   Give them referrals anyway.
10. People really need help but may attack you if you do help them.
    Help them anyway.
11. Give the world the best you have, and you'll sometimes get kicked in the teeth.
    Give the world the best you have anyway.
12. Some people won't ever really believe in the Universal Law of Reciprocity and will show in their body language that you're silly for believing in it. Some won't care that this is a Biblical principle.
    Believe in the Universal Law of Reciprocity anyway.

Review and reflect on these paradoxical commandments prior to a networking event. They provide a poignant reminder of the challenges of sincerely desiring to become a fearless networker. You may receive unjust criticism and negative responses. When this happens, I recall one of Dale Carnegie's human relations principles from *How to Win Friends and Influence People,* a book that is timeless. "Unjust criticism is often a compliment in disguise." People who criticize unjustly are often jealous or envious of another's attitude, behavior or success. Enjoy these words of wisdom!

Quick Summary: 🐍

Even when you have the best intentions, you won't be immune to criticism from negative or self-centered people. Don't let the narrow-mindedness of a few people discourage you from being a "go-giver."

Objectives:

1. To focus on how you can help or contribute to a networking event even when confronted by negative people
2. To remember the Dale Carnegie principle, "Unjust criticism is often a compliment in disguise"

Action Plan:

1. Review and reflect on the Paradoxical Commandments of Fearless Networkers (PCFN) when you are feeling discouraged or unappreciated in your networking efforts.
2. Give yourself a self-affirmation talk prior to a networking event or meeting. Keep focused on helping or making a contribution.
3. Conduct a post interview analysis using the Fearless Networkers' Interview Checklist found in Chapter 18.
4. Conduct a $+\triangle$ analysis to ascertain how well you followed the PCFN and what could you change or improve for a better result.

Fearless Networker's Interview Checklist

"Once we accept our limits we go beyond them."

-Brenden Francis

Conducting an assessment of your performance soon after a networking meeting is a vital component of business networking. The following questions will help with this assessment:

- Did I make the prospective referral feel at ease by asking rapport-building questions?
- Did I ask mostly closed-ended questions? (questions that elicit yes or no responses)
- Did I ask penetrating-questions about concerns? (who, what, when, where, why and how)
- Did I get behavioral examples to assist understanding the scope of the problem or need?
- Did I record specifics of the examples? (names, dates, numbers, locations or times)
- Did I get enough information to identify members in my network who might help?
- Did I allow time for silence so referral would have adequate time to respond?
- Did I listen to the prospect much more than I talked about my products and services?
- Did I have the prospect prioritize his or her issues out of the ones mentioned?

- Did I follow closely, the **A.L.T.E.R.** and **P.L.I.E.R.S.** tracts?
- Did I introduce someone in my network for products and services I don't provide?
- Did I exchange business cards at the end of the conversation?
- Did I set up a meeting for a network member and myself to attend with the interviewee?

Quick Summary: 💡

Conducting a post interview analysis is an important tool in your tool kit. The analysis helps you stay on target.

Objectives: 💡

1. To develop a habit of conducting a post interview checkup
2. To devote yourself to continuous improvement

Action Plan: 💡

1. Keep blank copies of this post interview checklist in your car.
2. Review and reflect on the just completed interview.
3. Conduct the post interview analysis.
4. Strive to improve in the areas you omitted or you were weak.
5. Use the post interview checklist to assist you in completing a $+\triangle$ analysis. Identify what went well and what you could change or improve to have a better result.

Chapter 19

Small Steps That Lead to Exceptional Networking

> *"If you have great ambition, take as big a step as possible in the direction of fulfilling it. The step may only be a tiny one, but trust that it may be the largest one possible for now."*
>
> -Mildred McAfee

Following the ideas in "Small Steps that Lead to Exceptional Networking" will establish your reputation as a fearless networker devoted to business development. Most important is taking each step of the networking tract. Failing to apply each of these steps will compromise your success as a fearless networker. The rewards of achieving your goals as a networker are explained by the motto: "Givers Gain."

Exceptional Networking Tips:

1. Consistently make opportunities to ask your circle of influence*, "Who do you know who has recently expressed a need for _____(Product/Service)_____?"
2. Have attractive, well-kempt business cards. Avoid handing out worn, tattered, or used business cards.
3. Promptly follow up on referrals given you by your network. Keep the member informed throughout the relationship building process.
4. Regularly give referrals to your network especially when you are personally in need of a member's product or service. Being a customer yourself is one of the best ways to determine the level of customer service your referrals will be receiving.
5. Keep your Personal Digital Assistant (PDA) file and your manual business card file up to date with current information. Automated contact information systems are now available to periodically request updates to contact information via email.
6. Respond to requests for assistance or information preferably the same day or no later than the next business day. How a network member responds to a request for assistance is a key indication of how much the network member values the relationship.

7. If you are on vacation or out of town, use the auto-return messenger on your e-mail and phone system.
8. Show your commitment to help your network grow their businesses. Consistently ask, "How can I help you grow your business today? Are you promoting any specials this month?"
9. Keep your network in the forefront of your thinking. When in front of a prospective referral, be ready to recommend a member of your network.
10. Show your interest in your network members businesses. Participate in special events put on by members of your network. Examples are trade-show booth displays, public seminars, Chamber ribbon-cutting ceremonies and client socials.
11. Join several networking groups that excel at referral sharing to expand your network of people marketing your services.
12. Join professional groups of a different culture than yours. Exceptional networkers understand the bottom line value of networking to groups that demographically mirror their client base. For example, I also belong to the Asian Chamber of Commerce and to Hispanic and African American Professional Consortiums.
13. Send all personalized thank you cards and notes via snail mail.

Quick Summary: 💡

The most important asset you have as a networker is your reputation. A fearless networker is committed to the success of the people in his/her network. High levels of professionalism are evident throughout the relationship building process.

Objectives: 💡

1. To ask your circle of influence, "Who do you know in your ___ (club, business, firm, or service organization) that has a need for _____ (product/service)?"
2. To expand your base of marketers of your products or services by joining several groups committed to referral sharing.

Action Plan:

1. Adopt the scouting motto, "Be Prepared" to network.
2. Keep your network member informed about the status of the referral.
3. Utilize the principles "Small Steps that Lead to Exceptional Networking" with prospective referrals.
4. Send prospective referrals thank you cards and notes via snail mail. Although e-mails are quicker, handwritten notes and thank you cards are still considered proper business etiquette.
5. Conduct a +△ analysis each time you consciously use the principles f the "Ten Steps to Exceptional Networking." Ascertain what went well and what could have been improved or changed through the use of these principles.

*Circle of Influence = Co-workers, family members, church/synagogue/mosque/temple/kingdom hall members, social clubs, sororities/fraternities, professional associations, networking groups, doctor/dentist/chiropractics offices, barber/ beauty and nail salons

"Dancing" or meeting with a member in your network, is absolutely the best way to learn what you need to know to help each other find the most profitable prospective clients and to develop an "equal trade" arrangement

Chapter 20

Dancing with Those That "Brung" You

"I do for you, maybe one day you do for me"
-Robin Williams, as Joey O'Brien in "Cadillac Man"

"Dancing" is an important part of networking! A "dance" is a meeting between two network members. Usually this takes place at a member's office, a conveniently located restaurant, possibly for coffee, breakfast or lunch. The meeting is designed so members can learn about each other's product or service and to provide an "equal trade" arrangement where both can help each other, in the future, by sharing referrals. You can assess each other's commitment to service. You can plan to build a foundation based on trust and respect. Hopefully, you will become more comfortable with each other. In addition, you can establish the uniqueness of products or services and any competitive edge. You may become aware of people in your circle of influence that may perhaps utilize the services or products of your "dance" partner. "Dancing," will allow you to coach your "dance" partner on how to best know, find and approach your most profitable prospective client and with the "equal trade" arrangement in mind, allow the same for your "dance" partner. A "dance" is one of the best opportunities to ask for a referral or at least to say, "Here's how you can help me." However, you must be specific in describing your most profitable prospective referral and telling why this person would need your product or service.

After every dance, I leave with a clearer picture of at least one prospective referral to pre-qualify for my "dance" partner. For example, I recently "danced" with Ron Schowe, owner of Nushow Computers at his new office location. After a brief tour, we sat and discussed the Lan Center.

He had 31 high-speed Internet stations for Combatx games, popular with teens and young adults. During the meeting, we brainstormed ways to bring in groups of teens to the Lan Center. I am involved with teen groups through my Rotary club. I immediately thought of four (4) teen groups that I could speak with about the Lan Center. After my meeting with Ron, I contacted each group leader of the four groups. I promoted the Lan Center with flyers Ron's wife Jan had tailored for the teen groups. As a result, I created interest in having each group come in for a "lock-in" at Nushow Computers.

Before I visited Ron Schowe's new office, I knew little about his Lan Center. Therefore, I could not speak intelligently about this new part of Ron's business. Over a two-week period, I generated four "hot" referrals for my fellow network member, Ron Schowe. Following is the information sheet that I used to gather important data to promote my fellow network members and their products or services. Before "dancing" with a fellow network member, I gather basic knowledge of my "dance" partner's business from the 60 seconds product or service presentation.

Have fun "dancing" with your business network members!

Dance Information Sheet

Dance Partner's Name: _____ Date:___/___/___

Dance Partner's Company's Name: _____

I. What products or services do you specialize in? List no more than 3 or 4.

_____

_____

_____

II. What are the main demographics of your client-base? Consider individuals, age, gender, income range, business type, size, small, mid-size or large, number of employees.

_____

_____

III. What key attributes or value-added qualities separate you or your company from the competition? Consider success factors, such as, exceptional customer care, flexible scheduling, fast turnaround time, personalized service.

_____

_____

IV. What story can you relate that exemplifies the attributes or value added qualities mentioned above that *you* provide? Highlight in 30 words or less.

_____

_____

V. Who is your most profitable prospective client and where will I most likely find him or her?

_____

_____

VI. What situation would compel a prospective referral to want or need your product?

_____

_____

VII. How would you recommend I approach your most profitable prospective referral?

_____

_____

VIII. Please highlight key information in your product/service brochure for me to show prospective referrals. Highlight key product features and benefits, major accomplishments/awards (use a pen with red ink).

Permission to copy this "Dance Information Sheet" as a part of a networking one-on-one meeting is granted by Fearless Networking. Any other use is strictly prohibited.

96

Quick Summary: 💡

The best way to learn more about your network members' products or services is, to have a "dance" with them at a pre-determined meeting place. "Dancing" allows adequate time to uncover details about each partner's product, service and organization.

Objectives: 💡

1. To set up at least two "dances" weekly with a different member of your network
2. To utilize the "Dance Information Sheet" provided in this chapter at every "dance"
3. To ask pertinent questions so you can properly promote the products or services of your network
4. To use the "Dance Information Sheet" to ask for help in finding pre-qualified prospective referrals
5. To use the "Dance Information Sheet" to teach a network member how to market your product or service.

Action Plan: 💡

1. Set up a "dance" with a network member this upcoming week.
2. Interview your "dance" partner using the "Dance Information Sheet."
3. Conduct a $+\triangle$ analysis of what went well with your "dance." Also determine what you would improve or change for a better result.

Chapter 21

Review and Write Up after Initial Contact at Networking Event

"Whenever you do a thing, act as if all the world were watching."

-Thomas Jefferson

Establish a contact record listing to discuss prospective referral with a network member you have selected. You may enter information in your electronic database system. Or since you are giving the referral to a network member, a manual contact sheet should suffice. See the attached example contact record.

Reminders:
    Under needs, issues and concerns:

> ➢ The needs as expressed by the prospective referral, for example, time saved providing payroll services
> ➢ The names of other key company personnel mentioned

Other information:

    # Clients/customers
    # Employees
    Size of company
    Type of customers serviced
    Who is currently doing your payroll?

Any additional statements made by contact in jest or that may seem irrelevant:

> For example:
>> Boy, we need that service at our company, just kidding!
>> My boss really needs to talk to you; we have problems!
>> I don't think our current bookkeeper is that sharp, just joking!
>> My boss really needs training he/she is terrible with financial issues.

The Contact Record Form

Contact's (Referral's) Name:

Position/Title:

Company Name:

Company Address:

Company Phone: **Fax:**   **Email:**   **Web:**

-Date: **Location of Initial Meeting with Prospective Referral:**

-Needs/Concerns Expressed:

-Facts/Parties Involved:

-Additional Statements:

Example Contact Record

Contact's Name: Shelly Hanes

Position/Title: Office Manager

Company Name: Entertainment Ideas, Inc.

Company Address: Post Office Box 571778
(6000 Kirby Avenue)
Houston, Texas 77257

Company Phone: xxx-xxx-xxxx Fax: xxx-xxx-xxxx Email: info@xx.org
Web: www.xx.org

Date: **Location of Initial Meeting with Referral Given You:**

8/27/03 **Galleria Area Chamber**

Needs/Concerns Expressed:
Shelly mentioned that Elsa (our only) customer service rep is doing the payroll. Every two weeks she spends about 3-4 hours preparing to run payroll on our Quick Books system. Our CPA Alex Villarreal does the quarterly 941 reporting.
Elsa needs to focus solely on customer service work. Every time she takes time to run payroll, we have customer service issues that don't get handled.
Our CPA Alex is usually late filing the 941 reports causing us to pay a late penalty. In addition, I have checked with other CPA's in my Rotary club and found that we're paying Alex about $200 more than they would charge.

Other Facts/Parties Involved:
I was introduced to Shelly by a fellow BNI member, David Sharp at a Galleria Area Chamber of Commerce (GACC) event.

Shelly attended the GACC luncheon with Mary Flores (Anna on business card), marketing manager at Cozumel Liquor Stand on Kirby (6000

Kirby). Her phone # is xxxxxxx. She invited me to come by and talk with her.

Additional Information:
12 clubs with approximately 50 employees each.
1--(P/T) Bookkeeper/Customer Service Rep

Quick Summary: 💡

As soon as possible after attending a networking meeting, enter the information gathered in an electronic database system (Contact Management Software) like ACT!, Goldmine, Maximizer, and TELEmagic.

Objective: 💡

1. To establish a detailed accounting of the initial contact with a prospective referral
2. To include needs, issues and concerns

Action Plan: 💡

1. Review highlighted information jotted on reverse side of business card. Fill out a contact record as soon as you return from the networking event. If you delay even one day, you can lose, as much as, 40% retention after 24 hours.
2. Use a manual Contact Record Form or electronic database to capture key information.
3. Conduct a $+\triangle$ analysis to ascertain what went well in documenting the initial contact. Ascertain what you could improve or change for a better result.

Chapter 22

Selling Versus Business Networking

"Better to be prepared and not have an opportunity than to have an opportunity and not be prepared."

-Les Brown

Sales, is a profession with high income potential second only to the medical profession in average annual income. However, selling is not the same as business networking. Selling is more inward focused where the professional salesperson is focused on meeting her personal needs, such as monthly quota, sales activity goals, appointments scheduled, presentations made, etc. There is certainly nothing wrong with being a goal oriented salesperson. There is a critical need for more focused, goal achieving salespeople. They are the backbone of any company. When you don't sell anything or if your expenses exceed your sales revenue, you won't be in business very long. Business networking, on the other hand, is outward focused. The business networker sees her customer or prospect as more than a person with money. She sees the customer or prospect as a person with needs. The business networker is focused more on the entire business not just the area where there is a need for her product or service. The customer or prospect usually has other needs that the business networker can not meet with the product or services being provided. However, there may be others in his network that could meet the other needs expressed by the customer or prospect. Hopefully, there are people in her network that are returning the favor and are touting her product or service to their customers or prospects. There are several definitions of business networking that clearly explain this relationship difference (See Chapter 1):

Business networking is:

- Acquiring a database of diverse people with diverse products and services who understand and practice "give and take"
- Compiling a list of people you can count on
- Relationship building with the intent to eventually share referrals

As a salesperson, at a networking event, when your focus is on your needs only (e.g., meeting quotas, getting appointments) you come across as needy and neediness repels. As a salesperson when you focus on how you can help or contribute by meeting the needs of those attending the networking event (even those needs outside the scope of the product or service you offer) you come across as caring and caring attracts. You are suddenly taking a big step towards transforming into an effective relationship manager; a true business networker!

Once you become focused on the total needs of your customer and actively seek to provide solutions to their problems through the products and services of members of your network, you become an invaluable asset that is likely to be in a long term confidant-type relationship that most competitors can not threaten. 70% of my customers have been with me at least seven (7) years.

A question the reader could be asking herself after reading up to this point, "Can I be both an effective business networker and an effective salesperson?" The answer is a resounding yes! The difference is mainly an attitude change. A change in how you view a customer or prospect. The better question is, "Do I view my customer or prospect as a person in need that I want to help or do I view him as a person who can meet my needs?" The answer to this question can mean whether you can have sustaining long term profitable relationships or be in a position to constantly have to find your next sale just to maintain status quo.

Selling	*Business Networking*
1. More inward focused on meeting personal quotas	1. More outward focused on contributing or helping
2. Focused on the need for my products or services	2. More focused on any need expressed
3. Compiling a list of prospects to sell to.	3. Compiling a list of people I can count on.

4. Mainly view prospects as people who can possibly meet my needs (buy my products)

4. Mainly view prospects as people I can help

5. Focused on my products when listening for needs

5. Focused on my network when listening for needs

Quick Summary:

There is a big difference between selling and business networking. The difference can be determined by what the person is focused on when communicating with the prospect.

Objectives:

1. To have a balance in your networking and selling. A good rule of thumb is 60% networking and 40% selling
2. To focus on your network associates when listening for needs
3. To compile a list of people you can count on (networking)

Action Plan:

1. Set aside an uninterrupted block of time to prepare for the upcoming sales or networking meeting. Rule of thumb: preparation time is three times the time spent in presentation. For example, a 30 minutes presentation would take about 90 minutes to prepare.
2. Rehearse your presentation using a tract provided in this manual, such as the "Pre-qualifying referrals (**P.L.I.E.R.S.**)" tract.
3. Use a tape recorder to rehearse your presentation.
4. Be sure voice tone shows that you're genuinely interested in helping the referral fill a need.
5. Prepare a tailored self-affirmation talk as preparation for the upcoming meeting.
6. Conduct a $+\triangle$ analysis of your practice or rehearsal session. Ascertain what went well and what you could change for a better result.

Chapter 23

How Fearless Networkers Have More Long-Term Relationships

"We are what we repeatedly do. Excellence then, is not an act, but a habit."

-Aristotle

Fearless networkers start to build long-term relationship at the moment they make a connection with a prospective referral. From that point on fearless networkers build relationships that have a foundation of trust, mutual respect and understanding. Following is a list of strategies fearless networkers use to help build long-term, confidante relationships:

1. While the referral, who is now a client of your network associate, is happily involved in using the product or service of your network associate schedule a meeting to determine how you may further contribute or help.

2. Host a monthly or quarterly executive breakfast and invite the client to come and meet your clients and members of your network to learn about each other's businesses and explore how referrals may be shared.

3. During the meeting make sure you allow time for the attendees who are currently doing business with each other to give testimonials of the benefits they are obtaining as a result of their business relationships.

4. For introductions, use the "60 Seconds Introduction Form" found on page 55 of the Fearless Networking book. Give attendees 3 minutes to fill out form at the same time.

5. Use the "Dance Information Sheet" found on page 96 of the Fearless Networking book, to learn how to market each other's products and services. Give the attendees three (3) minutes to

complete the "Dance Information Sheet." Then conduct a "speed networking" session to allow each attendee five (5) minutes to share key marketing information with another attendee to help in referral sharing process. After 5 minutes move to next person.

6. Regularly send articles to the referral client or your client that relates to the business needs, issues and concerns mentioned in your initial meeting. A great source of articles is in the business section of the ISP newsletter or the Internet search link.

7. Establish a consultant-type relationship with your client or referral client and actively pursue the next engagement during each consultation visit. Use the A.L.T.E.R. tract and the P.L.I.E.R.S. tract found on pages 40 and 73 respectively to pre-qualify the client for your or your network's products and services.

8. Refer the service of your network associates in fresh areas your client or referral client hasn't been exposed to.

9. Create alliances with other consultants and allow them to jump-start new projects toward the end of current engagements you have with existing clients.

10. When making a presentation to an existing client it is highly recommended that you stand and deliver the presentation. (See the next page for reasons why).

11. Once a referral client becomes your personal client, ask to be invited to in-company strategy sessions to provide an outsider's perspective and, if need be, give referrals to help with current needs, issues, concerns and opportunities discussed in the strategy sessions. Be willing to sign a Non-Disclosure Agreement, if requested to do so.

When dancing with a "dance" partner (See step 5 above), remember your "dance" partner should be equally as enthusiastic about helping you grow your business. Remember, never to ask a referring member to give you a referral in return for one you have given. This violates the "Law of Reciprocity" and the "equal trade" arrangement. Just say enthusiastically,

"Here's how you can help me grow my business." Then you bring out the Dance Information Sheet!

If practical, I strongly recommend a face-to-face stand up presentation.

Stand Up and Deliver!
A controlled study concerning, the impact of presentations was conducted by the Wharton School of Business at the University of Pennsylvania. Two groups were given presentations to do. The objective was to persuade people to invest their money in a new business. The presentations contained the same numbers, facts and statistics. The presentations were the same with two exceptions. One presenter gave the presentation sitting down, talking across a table. The other presenter delivered their presentation standing up, using visual aids.
The results were interesting. The group sitting down and talking was able to convince 58% of the people to say, "I will sign up for that business proposition," The second group was able to get 79% of their audience to say, "I will sign up for this proposition." When the second group was surveyed, they felt that the person who stood up and used visual aids appeared more credible, more interesting, better prepared and more professional. (See *"Presentations Plus"* by David A. Peoples, for more help with preparing winning presentations).

In another controlled study conducted by the University of Minnesota with similar parameters, the results revealed that if you stand up and give a presentation using visual aids, your client, or your prospect, is 43% more likely to be persuaded. However, an unexpected and unanticipated outcome came out of this study. If you stand up and give a presentation using visual aids, your client or prospect will be willing to pay 26% more money for the same product or service! Again, I implore you to conduct a stand up presentation in your proposal and action plan meeting.

Quick Summary: 💡

Begin with the end in mind and have a mindset that you want to build a long-term relationship with the client.

Objectives: 💡

1. To keep in regular contact with all clients through phone calls, mailed articles, and formal and informal meetings
2. To think about how you can help fill a need any time you are with your client or in communication with a client
3. To show a genuine concern and empathy for the client's needs, issues and concerns
4. To determine the next step in the process of building a long-term relationship, with the help of the client

Action Plan: 💡

1. Give yourself a pre-planned self-affirmation talk tailored before meeting with a client
2. Maintain a mind-set throughout the meeting that bespeaks an attitude of giving, "How can I help this client?" Avoid thinking, "What can I get?" or "What can this business contribute to my bottom-line?"
3. Review the above success strategies.
4. Use the "Success Tips for Smooth Sailing" in Chapter 23, to ascertain whether you covered the key success factors.
5. Conduct a $+\triangle$ analysis using the above success tips. Use the post network meeting interview checklist to help determine what went well and what could improve or change.

Chapter 24

Selecting the Right Business Networking group for You

> *"A genius with inadequate information is at a distinct disadvantage to an individual with average intelligence with superior information"*

> -Author Unknown

In my opinion, leaving a networking group to join another to reduce the amount of dues you pay is short-sighted. Even leaving because of a lack of referrals you are receiving could fall into the same category. Certainly, if the number of referrals being received by you is not covering your dues, there is a problem. It is then time to take an assessment but not the time necessarily to make a rash, uninformed decision to quit. To determine if you should move on to another networking group because of a lack of referrals, make sure you are not the reason for the lack of referrals. Have you done the following?

- Let your associates in your current networking group know what you are looking for
- Been specific and clear about what type of referral or contact you need
- Never demanded a referral in return for giving one. Used instead a gentle prod approach that allowed the associate to respond in a comfortable manner
- Told your associates where to find your most profitable, prospective referral
- And taught your associates how to greet and pre-qualify these prospective referral types

Following is a checklist of points to consider when looking for the right networking group:

- ➢ (Fool me once...) Visit the group twice before joining

➢ (Popular mechanic) Watch and listen closely for the type of referrals being exchanged. Don't be overly impressed by the numbers of referrals being exchanged. Joe, the mechanic, could be receiving 40% of the referrals because he's running a terrific special on oil changes.

➢ (Who says so besides you?) Are the members being supportive of each other by giving unprovoked raving testimonials of service after the sale they're receiving from those that they are doing business with in the group?

➢ (Dance Fever) Business Network International calls meeting during the week between the networking group meetings to learn more about each other's products, "dancing." If you're not dancing with your associates in your group on a regular basis, then you may not know enough about their products or services to comfortably market them through "word of mouth." Find out if the members are meeting with each other between formal group meetings to learn more about each other's products and services.

➢ (A catchy phrase) Are the members giving memorable, catchy phrases about their product or service at the end of their 60 seconds product introduction? This helps to recall associates PRODUCTS when in front of a prospective referral

➢ (A mind is a terrible thing to waste) Is your networking group providing new members an orientation soon after signing up? Also, are the members receiving weekly tips on how to effectively network from someone who has earned the right by example?

➢ (The proof is in the pudding) Are members providing testimonials from satisfied CLIENTS?

➢ (Getting my money's worth) Is the group keeping track of the dollar amount of referrals being given? Is it an impressive number?

➢ (The lone stranger) Are you the only guest today? A sure-fire sign of a growing prosperous networking group is the number of guests that are present at meetings.

➢ (Organization is a key leadership quality) Is the meeting run in an organized manner? A well run meeting is a sure-fire sign of a professional business networking group.

➢ (Recognition from the membership) At the end of the meeting are you being asked to give a brief (usually 15 seconds) comment about your impressions about the meeting and the members in attendance?

> (Join my team!) Are the members of the networking group eager for you to give consideration about joining the group? Is a professional prepared membership package available to take with you?

Quick Summary: 💡

Be observant of the members, number and type of referrals exchanged and the general atmosphere of the group when visiting.

Objectives:
1. To follow the checklists of key points provided above when visiting a new networking group.
2. To be observant and aware of what is happening in the group
3. To actively participate in a professional, respectful manner.

Action Plan: 💡

1. Give yourself a pre-planned self-affirmation talk tailored prior to attending a meeting of a new business networking group.

2. Maintain a mind-set throughout the meeting that bespeaks an attitude of giving. "How can I help this organization?" is better than "What can I get?" or "What can this group mean to my bottom-line?"

3. Review the bulleted items above and the "Success Tips for Smooth Sailing" from Chapter 23 to ascertain whether you covered the above checklist of points and the key success factors, respectively.

4. Conduct a $+\triangle$ analysis using the above success tips. Use the post network meeting interview checklist. Help determine what went well and what could improve or change for a better result.

5. Phone or e-mail the network member who invited you to the meeting. Give her a status report about your observations of the meeting. Thank her again for inviting you.

When you have achieved your networking goals, keep learning by reviewing the tracts and tips provided. Master networkers believe in and follow a continuous self-improvement program!

Happy Fearless Networking!

Post Self-Evaluation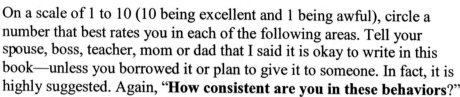

On a scale of 1 to 10 (10 being excellent and 1 being awful), circle a number that best rates you in each of the following areas. Tell your spouse, boss, teacher, mom or dad that I said it is okay to write in this book—unless you borrowed it or plan to give it to someone. In fact, it is highly suggested. Again, "**How consistent are you in these behaviors?**"

I desire to give to others much more than finding business for myself:
1   2   3   4   5   6   7   8   9   10

I actively listen for needs, issues and concerns when face-to-face with a prospect:
1   2   3   4   5   6   7   8   9   10

I reach out to others and am not a wallflower I do not loiter around the bar or food table:
1   2   3   4   5   6   7   8   9   10

I seek to build a relationship before delving into my product/opportunity spiel (I spend 90% of my time in rapport building, identifying common interests, needs identification and 5% on my own presentation):
1   2   3   4   5   6   7   8   9   10

I listen 80% and talk 20% when communicating with a prospective referral:
1   2   3   4   5   6   7   8   9   10

I think of my network when face-to-face with a prospective referral:
1   2   3   4   5   6   7   8   9   10

I work a room with poise and confidence:
1   2   3   4   5   6   7   8   9   10

I reach out to others to make a connection and am not just a card-dropper:
1   2   3   4   5   6   7   8   9   10

I am a **Fearless Networker!**
1   2   3   4   5   6   7   8   9   10

At the beginning of this work, you rated yourself prior to reading and using this manual. Please note the similarities and differences in your scores. More importantly, notice your growth as a networker using the time tested principles in this manual. Congratulations and go give!

Summary

Fearless Networking! Your action plan to mastering business networking!
The practical tools and techniques are in convenient, easy to use and
remember formats. The material is designed to aid recall and retention and
contains the following memory boosters:

- Motivational Sayings
- Short Introductions
- Quick Summaries
- Key Objectives
- Action Plans
- Acronyms
- Stacking Objects Mind-Pictures
- A Standard Index that Includes a Tracts and Tips Index
- Pre- and Post- Self Evaluations
- Reflection and Evaluation Guidelines
- Repetition of key words/phrases, such as, "Listen 80% of the time;
  talk 20% of the time, by asking the right questions."

You are ready to network at a moment's notice. If you are a shy and timid
networker, you have a complete system to become a more assertive,
courageous and successful networker. This resource manual provides
beginners and professionals with inspiration, self-direction and self-
discipline. You now can build an ever-expanding network of mutually
beneficial relationships via "word-of-mouth" marketing. Your business
network will reward you and your network with more money, inner joy
and satisfaction. You and your network will have increased market
penetration to remain competitive in the new millennium!

Become a Fearless Networker, By Being a Go-Giver!

BIBLIOGRAPHY

The Joy of Service! by Ron McCann as told by Joe Vitale. (1989, Service Information Source (SIS))

See You At The Top by Zig Ziglar. (1974, Pelican)

Dig Your Well Before You Become Thirsty by Harvey Mackay. (1999, Doubleday)

Selling For Dummies by Tom Hopkins. (1989, IDG Books)

How to Master the Art of Selling by Tom Hopkins.(1982, First Warner Books)

Presentations Plus by David A. Peoples. (1992, John Wiley & Sons (Second Edition))

Sales Scripts That Sell! by Teri Gamble and Michael Gamble. (1992, AMACOM)

The Life You Were Born To Live by Dan Millman. (1993, HJ Kramer, Inc.)

How To Win Friends and Influence People by Dale Carnegie. (1981, Simon & Schuster)

How To Stop Worrying and Start Living by Dale Carnegie. (1984, Simon & Schuster)

Soaring On The Wings Of Courage by Olayinka Joseph. (2002, Riverbank Books)

Networking Is Giving by Dave Sherman. (2003, Internet Article)

Take The Fear Out Of networking Events by Vickie Champion. (2003, Internet Article)

Masters of Networking by Ivan Misner and Dan Morgan. (2000, Bard Press)

How To Have More Than Enough by Dave Ramsey. *(2000, Penguin Books)*

People Smart by Tony Alessandra, Michael J. O'Connor with Janice Alessandra. (1990, Keynote Publishing Company)

Network of Champions by Shad Helmstetter. (1995, Chapel and Croft Publishing, Inc.)

The One Number You Need to Grow by Federick F. Reichheld, PhD (2003, Dec. Harvard Business Review)

People Power by Donna Fisher (1995, Bard Press)

Acknowledgements

Warmest thanks to Jerry Twentier, Ola Joseph, Gloria Smith, Reverend Chad Miller and Mary Williams for reading, reviewing and providing input to the early drafts of this book. Their comments and suggestions served in creating a clearer and more powerful manuscript.

Sandra Kuhlmann, Ph.D., provided outstanding editing and proofing support. I also want to thank Dr. Kuhlmann for her gracious and inspiring Foreword to this book.

Ken Burgess, The Final Factor, did a very commendable job in designing and developing the website for Fearless Networking! found at www.fearlessnetworkers.com.

Reverend Chad Miller, pastor of Spirit of Life Community Church provided spiritual support and advice on content. His weekly sermons, without fail, seemed to provide the inspiration for my next chapter.

Gloria Smith, a dear friend and advisor and the first female Deacon of Brentwood Baptist Church inspired me to write an entirely new chapter after I thought I had completed this book.

To Spirit of Life Community Church a small Church with a tremendously "big" heart. Thanks for your prayers and support.

To members of my Business Network International West-University Chapter, who helped with the "name my book contest." To the winning main title suggestion "Fearless Networking" submitted by Mary Harvey and her business partner J.D. Garner. To the winning subtitle suggestion "A Step-by-step Guide to Mastering Networking for Beginners and Professionals Even the Shy and Timid" submitted by L.A. "Tony" Kovach.

To the Educational Coordinators in my business networking group who, came before and after and who continue to inspire me: Helen Callier, Shelly Antley and Don Shelly.

Most importantly, I acknowledge you the reader. Purchasing this book proves that you desire to be a "go-giver" in service to others. You are committed to mutually supportive relationships. May you experience the joy and personal satisfaction I have received by contributing to others through Fearless Networking!

"Networking is making links from people we know to people they know, in an organized way, for a specific purpose, while remaining committed to doing our part, expecting nothing in return."

Donna Fisher

Dedication

I include in this dedication those outstanding organizations that helped shape my philosophy of giving, serving and contributing. These organizations include Dale Carnegie & Associates, Inc., The Executive Committee (TEC), Rotary International (RI), The Rotary Club of Sharpstown and Business Network International, Inc.

Fearless Networking! was made possible by my dear friends and business associates. Their professional, spiritual and financial support provides the resources so I can make a difference in other people's lives. Those individuals are Steve and Sarah Mathis, Ed and Nancy Loke, Karen Blakeman, Lovie Teague, Mary Jacquelyn Gallien, Valerie Washington, John Younker, Ron Marsh, Terrance Marsh, Rodney Green, Jon and Carolyn King, Reverend Chad Miller, David and Deborah Bergeron, Daisy Morales, Kathleen Mathy, Sheila Howieson, Donald Hanks, Curtis and Doris Gill, George and Beverly Yeiter, Chuck Monteith, Chad Greer, Jim and Marilyn Gardner, Steve and Sonya Kruse, Richard Rosenthal, Don and Divina Moore, Jeffrey and Desiree McLemore, Vaqar Naqvi, Larry and Joe-Ann Bates, Vee Smith, Mary Hamilton, Mary Milton, Bryant and Robin Banes, Jay and Dixie Sorkin, Ann Wright, D' Lisa Simmons, Al Balzer, Ed Nasta, Linda Gibson, Max Reichenthal, John Peter, Rob Degeyter, Keith Remels, Wendy Buscop, Joe Greenberg, Jimmy Cox, Craig Moore, Mary Harvey, Shelly Antley, Linda Hale, Larry Hooker, David Trifon, Jeff Novy, Gloria Smith, Anthony and Clara Marsh, Ronald M. Marsh, Lillian Marie Marsh, Jennifer Jacobs, Helen Callier, Gloria L. McCalister, Denton Bryant, Dr. Katherine Miller, Karen Howard, Margie Suarez, Bill and Barbara Singletary, Maurice and Wilhemina Zakhem, Zack Zakhem, Sandra Kuhlmann, Rick Jones, Ivan Misner, Donna Fisher and Bill Pellerin. A special dedication goes to my immediate and extended family.

In Memory of:

Linda Pruitt, my Executive Assistant

Charles "Chuck" Kaiser, Jr.-TEC Associates Round Table (T.A.R.T.)

Robert "Bob" Fitts, Past District Governor (Rotary 5890), Rotary Club of Sharpstown

Paul Hall, Rotary Club of Sharpstown

Joseph W. Marsh, oldest brother

Alfred L. Marsh, Jr., next oldest brother

Index

A

accountability, as Fearless Networker trait, 10–11
acronyms, as memory technique, 6
action plan and +Δ analysis
    attitudes of Fearless Networkers, 44
    behaviors of Fearless Networkers, 44
    business card utilization, 66–67
    business networking mistakes, 79–80
    contacts, 102
    dancing, 97
    excellence in giving referrals, 84
    exceptional networking small steps, 91
    Fearless Networker attitude, 44
    Fearless Networker behavior, 49
    "hot" referrals, 70–71
    initial meeting with referral, 109
    interviewer's checklist, 89
    Mackay Maxims, 64
    Marsh Mantra, 60–61
    mistakes, 79
    networking dos and don'ts, 34
    networking events, 24–25
    networking tract, 37, 42
    opportunity awareness, 52
    Paradoxical Commandments of Fearless Networking, 87
    philosophy of networking, 19–20
    pre-qualifying referrals, 76
    preparations for referral meeting, 105
    proposal and action plan presentation, 112
    referral, initial meeting with, 109
    referral, meeting preparations, 105
    referrals, "hot," 70–71
    self-affirmations, 29–30
    self-evaluation of networking performance, 89
    60 second presentation, 58
    small steps in networking, 91–92
active listening. see listening
affirmations and self-talk, 26–30, 82, 104–105

Fromm, Erich, 32

pre-qualifying referrals, 73–80, 82–84
preparation for meeting
    initial, with referral, 103–105
    proposal and action plan meeting, 110–112
presentations
    60 second presentation, 37, 54–58, 107
    30 second elevator speech, 54, 57
probing questions, 36, 50, 51, 69, 70, 78, 83, 89, 91
procrastination, avoiding, 8
Project Hope of Houston, 16

Q
qualifying questions, 65, 104
questions
    A.L.T.E.R. Tract, 40–41
    business card utilization, 65
    "hot" referrals, 69–71
    mistakes in business networking, 78
    pre-qualifying referrals, 73–80, 82–84
    for referral meeting, 104
questions types
    clarifying, 40, 104
    close-ended, 88
    follow-up, 32, 72, 78
    open-ended, 33, 37, 88
    penetrating, 40, 78, 88
    pre-planned, 47, 107, 109
    probing, 36, 50, 51, 69, 70, 78, 83, 89, 91
    qualifying, 65, 104
    rapport building, 88

R
reciprocity, law of, 10–11, 19, 60, 77, 108
referral, initial meeting with, 103–109
    preparation for, 103–105
    review and write up after, 98–102
    tips for, 106–109
referrals
    business networking mistakes, 77–80
    Contact Record Form, 100–102

tracts and tips, prior to networking event

Fax orders: 713-271-5516   **Send this form.**

Telephone orders: Call 832-368-4434
        Have your credit card ready.

E-mail Orders: info@fearlessnetworkers.com or Kenpm50@aol.com
Postal Orders: 11152 Westheimer #660 Houston, TX 77042-3222

Please send the following books, mini-books, CDs, audiotapes.

_____

_____
_____
_____
_____

Please send more information on:
☐ Other Books   ☐ Speaking/Seminars   ☐ Consulting (Group) ☐ Consulting (One-on-One) ☐ Interviews

Name:_____
Address:_____
City_____State_____ Zip_____
Telephone:_____
E-mail Address:_____
Please add 8.25% for products shipped to Texas addresses

Shipping by Air:
U.S.: $4.00 for first book, mini-book, CD or audiotape and $2.00 for each additional
product (estimate).

International: $9.00 for first book, mini-book, CD or audiotape and $5.00 for each
additional product (estimate).

Payment: $17.95 (Texas residents add $1.48 tax, total $19.43) ☐ Check ☐ Credit Card:
☐ Visa   ☐ MasterCard   ☐ AMEX   ☐ Discover

Card number:_____
Name on card:_____Exp. Date:_____

For a secured site for credit card or check payment, go to our website at
www.fearlessnetworkers.com